THE BOOK LOVER'S GUIDE TO
VENICE

In loving memory of E. Ann Gray

THE BOOK LOVER'S GUIDE TO

VENICE

RACHAEL MARTIN

WHITE OWL
AN IMPRINT OF PEN & SWORD BOOKS LTD.
YORKSHIRE – PHILADELPHIA

First published in Great Britain in 2026 by
White Owl
An imprint of
Pen & Sword Books Ltd.
Yorkshire - Philadelphia

Copyright © Rachael Martin, 2026

ISBN 978 1 03611 195 3

Printed and bound in India by Replika Press Pvt. Ltd.
Design: SJmagic DESIGN SERVICES, India.

The Publisher's authorised representative in the EU for product safety is Authorised Rep Compliance Ltd., Ground Floor, 71 Lower Baggot Street, Dublin D02 P593, Ireland.
www.arccompliance.com

For a complete list of Pen & Sword titles please contact

PEN & SWORD BOOKS LIMITED
George House, Beevor Street, Off Pontefract Road, Hoyle Mill, Barnsley, South Yorkshire, England, S71 1HN.
E-mail: enquiries@pen-and-sword.co.uk
Website: www.pen-and-sword.co.uk

or

PEN AND SWORD BOOKS
1950 Lawrence Rd, Havertown, PA 19083, USA
E-mail: uspen-and-sword@casematepublishers.com
Website: www.penandswordbooks.com

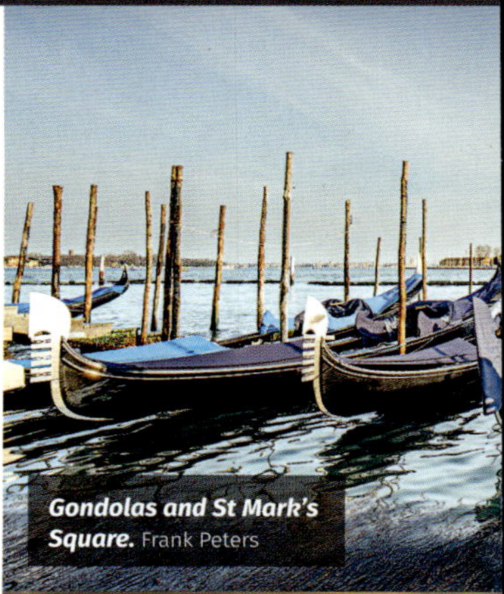

Gondolas and St Mark's Square. Frank Peters

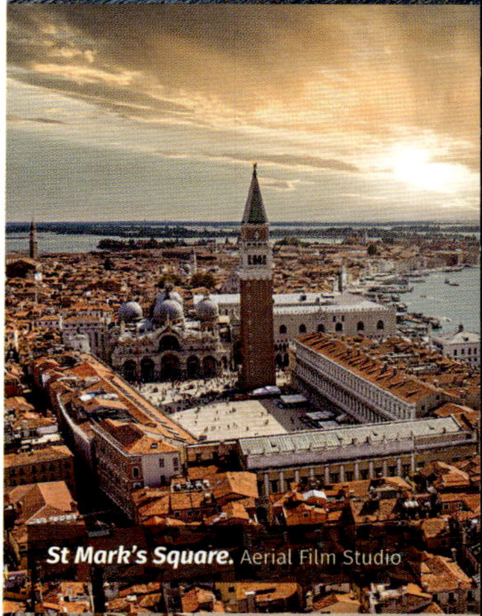

St Mark's Square. Aerial Film Studio

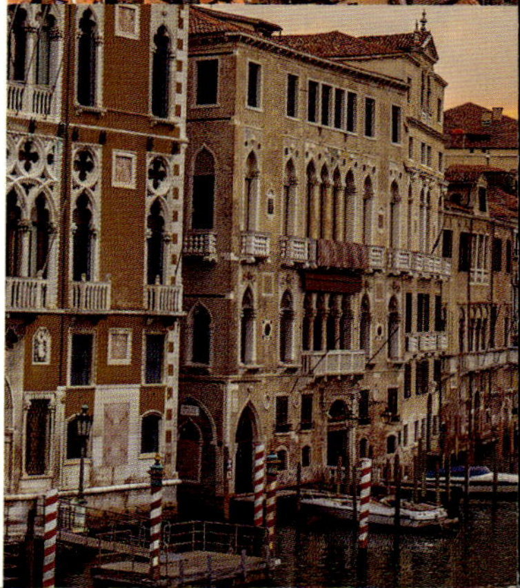

CONTENTS

Sunrise in Venice. Pattanasak Suksri

FOREWORD

The world may not have Venice and its lagoon islands to marvel at forever, for the archipelago sinks about one quarter inch every year. According to scientists, it will be underwater by 2150 as the wet ground beneath it and a gradual rise in sea levels slowly compacts its foundations over time. Of course, no one is more aware of its vulnerability than native Venetians. A pragmatic people of merchant stock, they will tell you themselves that their watery city, which seems to defy the very laws of nature, should be enjoyed to the fullest now, and for as long as it exists.

Founded some 1,600 years ago in a hidden lagoon enclosed between the water and the sky, glittering *Venezia*, from the Latin *Veni etiam*, 'return again', arises majestically from its very own little sea, once a swamp, surrounded by 118 islands and laced with some 150 canals. It is, in the words of art historian Giulio Lorenzetti in his 1926 tome *Venice and its Lagoon*, 'risen as if by a miracle out of the water that surrounds it and that like green shining ribbons, cut through its beautiful body'. *La Serenissima*, 'the most serene [one]',

as the Republic was dubbed long ago, has astonished, dazzled, flummoxed, beguiled and seduced all who have seen it. For centuries, countless books celebrated and reverenced its wonders until Henry James, in 1909, in his book of travel essays about Italy, *Italian Hours*, mused if there was anything to add.

Indeed there is and there will always be, as the marvel that is Venice continues to fascinate and astonish, even – and especially – in modern times. In this slim volume, Rachael

Julia della Croce. Photo courtesy of Julia della Croce

Martin has written a guide to Venice that is unique among travel books. In its pages, the reader can see Venice through the prism of great writers to experience its wonders not only through their words, but also through their imaginations.

'Nothing in the world that you have ever heard is equal to [its] magnificent and stupendous reality,' wrote Charles Dickens when he visited Venice in 1844. About the Lido, one of the lagoon islands that became a chic beach resort in the late nineteenth century frequented by the rich and famous, Shelley wrote '[The evening skies are] brighter than burning gold.' Whether Thomas Mann, D.H. Lawrence, Ernest Hemingway, Somerset Maugham, Nancy Mitford, or Daphne du Maurier, and so many more august voices, author Rachael Martin will tell you what they said –and, perhaps, what they did. Her book is filled with delicious stories and fun facts. Did you know, for example, that Venetian courtesans once glided along the canals in gondolas, bare-breasted and with pearls around their necks, or leaned out of their palazzo windows, likewise bare-breasted, to advertise their wares? Or, that the legendary fashion designer Coco Chanel was the first to popularise the suntan after catching too much sun on a Mediterranean cruise – and subsequently invented the one-piece swimsuit that became the rage on the beaches of the Lido to show it off? In this little volume you'll learn suchlike, and also trace the steps of the literati and cognoscenti, the famous and the infamous who visited and travelled there. And you can even descend upon the same cafés and bars where they met, caroused, ate and drank.

Whether planning a real trip to Venice or curling up in an armchair for a virtual tour, *The Book Lover's Guide to Venice* will make the journey even more fun. After initial historical notes and practical advice about the best time of year to go and how to plot a course upon arrival, the rest of the book is organised into three sections that will take readers beyond the well-travelled tourist routes, all the while annotating with bits of literary lore and historical sketches. *Buon viaggio!*

Julia della Croce

PREFACE

So why write a book about Venice, you might ask? As Henry James points out at the beginning of *Italian Hours* (1909), is there anything to add? Over the centuries writers have written about Venice many times. I wrote this book for two reasons. I love Venice and I love literature and reading. It gave me the chance not only to go back to Venice but also to the books and the stories and to discover new ones along the way, to bring it all together to create a picture of writers in Venice over the years. I've had the joy of writing the bits I enjoyed most into this slim volume that will easily fit into your handbag, coat pocket or back pocket of your jeans. It's the kind of book to take around with you as you discover Venice, or to enjoy one evening from the comfort of your armchair. This is the other thing. You don't even have to visit Venice as I hope that Venice will come to you as you read. I believe there are few greater pleasures in life, especially when it's cold and miserable outside.

You'll learn about well-known authors, authors that have gone off the radar for whatever reason over the years, and authors that haven't been written about much in English. You'll find Mary Shelley, the Romantic poets, Jan Morris, Donna Leon, Michael Dibdin, Henry James, Edith Wharton,

Gondolas with the island of San Giorgio Maggiore in the distance. rabbit75_fot

Ernest Hemingway, Patricia Highsmith, Muriel Spark, Nancy Mitford, Nancy Cunard, Lauren Elkin, Cynthia Zaran, Harriet Constable, Daphne du Maurier, society queens Lady Diana Cooper and Elsa Maxwell, radical women writers such as Lady Sydney Morgan and Moderata Fonte, early travel writers such as Marianna Starke, William Shakespeare, Virginia Woolf, Sylvia Pankhurst, Marco Polo, courtesans, political exiles, and more. You'll read about novels, memoirs, poetry, early travelogues, travel guides and biographies. You'll find contemporary historical novelists such as Tracy Chevalier and Michelle Lovric, and of course Casanova makes a star appearance, and not just for his highly documented sexual exploits, although admittedly that does have an awful lot to do with it. Besides, he certainly wasn't the only one, as you'll find out as you read on.

Sixteenth-century writer Francesco Sansovino was the author of *Venetia* (1581), one of the first guidebooks to Venice in Italian, a whole fourteen volumes of it. He tells us that Venice comes from the Latin *veni etia* or 'come again'. Henry James wrote that: 'The only way to care for Venice as she deserves it is to give her a chance to touch you often – to linger and remain and return.'[1] I hope, wherever possible, that you're inspired to do the same.

ACKNOWLEDGEMENTS

A big thank you to Jonathan Wright, Charlotte Mitchell, Janet Brookes and everyone at Pen & Sword Books. Many thanks to Barbara, Glenys, Jane and Rachel for reading, and to Stefano for making delicious things for me to eat at my desk.

1

HISTORICAL NOTES

Carnival in Venice. Marco

The End of the Republic

When Lord Byron went to Venice in 1816, the city had recently entered a new phase in its history. The Republic of Venice had fallen to Napoleon in 1797 when the city's last ruler or Doge, Ludovico Manin, abdicated.

La Serenissima, the most serene one as it was known, was no more. It had been founded over a thousand years before in 677. In its heyday it was the greatest of marine republics, a thriving trade centre and gateway to the east. Venice, in fact, was the meeting point for east and west, the city where the

The Republic of Venice flag with the lion of St Mark. Crisfotolux

west ended and the east began, and its streets were testimony to this, a whole mix of people and cultures, and spices on the market stalls that came from foreign lands. Yet by the eighteenth century, the trade had all but disappeared, the ruling aristocracy were ineffective,[1] and the city had become more known for its courtesans and its *ridotti* or gambling dens. Jan Morris wrote in *Venice* (1960): 'No wonder Napoleon swept her aside,'[2] while others saw the fall of the Republic as punishment for all the decadence.

Eighteenth-Century Venice

Eighteenth-century Venice was very attractive to foreigners. Young aristocrats on their Grand Tours, the traditional tour through Italy in search of art and culture, made the most of the city's freedoms and the opportunity to sexually indulge as they pleased. It was the city where 'enjoyment was the only art and life the only object of study'.[3]

Naturally the Venice Carnival was very popular with foreign aristocrats. They enjoyed the masked balls, fireworks, opera, and of course the courtesans.[4]

Riva degli Schiavoni, eighteenth-century print. Caifas

Carnival in Venice. Pietro D'Antonio

Masks were not only confined to carnival. People were allowed to wear them between October and Lent, minus the *Novena* or nine days before Christmas, which meant that all kinds of things could take place if your face was covered. English gentlemen also have the fame of taking sexually transmitted diseases back to Britain, where at the time there were no adequate treatments.[5] James Bowell, eighteenth-century author of *The Life of Samuel Johnson* (1791), was known for his liaisons with courtesans both at home and in Venice and is said to have had gonorrhoea at least nineteen times. Alongside all this, the eighteenth century gave us artistic treasures such as Goldoni's plays, Tiepolo's frescoes and Baldassare Galuppi's comic operas.[6] Galuppi also wrote music for the harpsichord, and Robert Browning writes of the power of his harpsichord music in his poem *A Toccata of Galuppi's* (1855).

How Napoleon, and not death, then took away a whole way of Venetian life from its eighteenth-century

protagonists is described beautifully at the end of Edith Wharton's *Italian Backgrounds* (1905). Wharton goes off to look for the Venice of the eighteenth century and finds it in the Correr Museum in the mannequins dressed in their robes yet stripped of their world. Jeanette Winterson sets her novel *The Passion* (1987) partially in Venice during the Napoleonic wars. It's the story of Henri, who works as Napoleon's cook and keeps him fed with chicken, and

The Grand Canal. Eyetronic

Villanelle, daughter of a Venetian boatman. They meet in Venice against the backdrop of the Napoleonic Wars and Venice herself, a city ripe for the fantastical world that Winterson creates.

A New Era

The fall of the Venetian Republic and the arrival of Napoleon with new laws heralded a modern era for Venice, which would later include a train and road to connect it to the mainland. The Napoleonic Wars (1803–15) had brought a stop to European travel. When they ended, it was safe to travel again, unless you were the Shelleys and had gone anyway. Percy Bysshe Shelley, Romantic poet, and Mary Shelley, soon to be author of *Frankenstein* (1818), eloped in 1815 and took Mary's stepsister Claire Clairmont with them. They didn't get to Italy, they'd have to wait a couple more years for that,

but they did travel around France and witnessed first-hand the devastation caused by war. When they got to Venice in 1818, some of the palazzos were in various states of disrepair but if you were a Romantic poet in possession of a creative mind, this air of decaying decadence merely helped feed your literary imagination. Obviously, the Venetians, having lived through war and the occupation of their city, took a very different view of it all.

The Venetian Salons

Venice attracted some of the greatest writers, poets and intellectuals of the nineteenth century. They rented, and in some cases bought, palazzos along the Grand Canal. The Republic had fallen, but Venice was becoming a cultural and intellectual capital. The writers involved continued the tradition of the *salotti veneziani*, what the French called *salons* or intellectual drawing rooms, which in Venice had originally developed from the *casini* or *ridotti* where the Venetians gathered to gamble. Now they gathered to discuss culture and the arts, and exchange ideas. During the seventeenth and eighteenth centuries, these meetings often took place in the homes of Venetian

Venice landscape in Veile, K. Human History (1896), St. Petersburg. wowinside

noblewomen. In the nineteenth century wealthy American women arrived and opened their drawing rooms. The pursuits were the same: culture, the arts, intellectual discussion, and naturally the social side of it all, too.

Destination Venice

Venice became a destination not just for the wealthy but also for the middle classes, and in 1868 Thomas Cook included it in his tours. His new tour of Italy included Venice,

MIT studio

Florence, Rome and Naples.[7] Two world wars stopped the foreign visitors and caused change, but Venice would remain both inspiration and destination, and in some cases provide exile, for writers from over the world. On 4 November 1966, Venice hit the headlines when there was a terrible sea flood. Writer Jan Morris points to this as the beginning of global interest in Venice.[8] The water level in the city rose by 196cm. For twenty-four hours the city was immersed by water, with no electricity or gas. It brought Venice to the world's attention and highlighted the possibility that one day the city might be lost.

Christine de Pizan

The first European woman to earn her living by her pen was Cristina da Pizzano, or Christine de Pizan as she became known. She was born in Venice in September 1364. Her father, Tommaso da Pizzano, was Professor of Medicine and Astrology at the University of Bologna, and in the same year that Cristina was born, he was summoned to the court of France. Cristina went to France when she was 4 years old. She became the first European woman to earn her living by her pen. Her *The Book of the City of Ladies* (1405) is considered by many to be the first protofeminist text in western history. We do not know her mother's name. She is remembered only as the daughter of Tommaso Mondini, an aristocratic advisor of the Venetian Republic, and was Venetian.

2

WHEN TO GO

I suggest you go in low season, roughly between November and March. It's easier then to imagine the Venice of the past, those masked figures in eighteenth-century dress darting through the streets on their way to some party or secret rendezvous, Henry James looking out over the Grand Canal, poet and courtesan Veronica Franco writing her verses before preparing herself to welcome a powerful patrician for the night, or Patricia Highsmith heading off for cocktails with art collector Peggy Guggenheim at Harry's Bar. Ernest Hemingway was also a regular at Harry's Bar and would sit there drinking Montgomery cocktails. Speaking of which, if you're reading from home, you could always try preparing the said cocktail before you read on or make yourself a spritz using the Venetian bitter Select. You might also want to look out Sybille Bedford's last essay *Venice in Winter* (1967) in her collection *Pleasures and Landscapes* (2003). 'Let us go there while we may,'[1] she ends, deeply aware of the fragility of the city.

Getting Around Venice

For Evelyn Waugh, 'The only way to appreciate Venice is on foot.'[2] Donna Leon loves the city's lack of cars, as walking causes you to meet people and make acquaintances based upon brief acknowledgements that nevertheless carry on for years.[3] Tom Ripley, in Patricia Highsmith's *The Talented Mr Ripley* (1955), also likes the fact that Venice has no cars. 'It made the city human. The streets were like veins, he thought, and the people were the blood, circulating everywhere.'[4] Venice is a city that lends itself to walking. It can be a bit overwhelming to navigate, especially if you're visiting for the first time. Lauren Elkin's *Flâneuse: Women Walk the City in Paris, New York, Tokyo, Venice and London* (2016) is about women who walked in cities. *Flâneuse* is the female form of the French word *flâneur*, a man who walks around cities, an observer rather than a participant. Elkin spent a month in Venice to research a novel she was writing and visited the Sophie Calle art exhibition 2007 Biennale di Venezia. Calle, whose name in Italian means street, followed a man from Paris to Venice, a city known for surveillance, following people and ultimately spying on them during the time of the Venetian Republic. Calle notes in her journal about how the city is like a labyrinth, and Elkin describes how she too gets lost. This happens in Venice, is all part of the adventure, and if you do get lost, well, you won't be the first.

Venice is a car-free zone, so the chances are you're either going to

be walking or getting on the public waterbus system known as the vaporetto boats, unless you decide to rent a gondola or private boat. If you decide to take the vaporetto, a day ticket or two-day ticket is often your cheapest option. Give yourself time. This is the last place in the world where you want to be rushing round. The city's beauty is best savoured slowly, so make sure you stop off at those cafés, find a bench, and just watch that Venetian world go by.

Venice's Districts

The Grand Canal is nearly 4km long and divides the city into two from near the Santa Lucia station to St Mark's Basin opposite St Mark's Square. The city is divided into *sestieri* or districts. The districts of Cannaregio, San Marco and Castello are to the north and Santa Croce, San Polo and Dorsoduro are to the south. Buildings within the *sestieri* are all numbered from one right up to the last house in the district. This makes for some high house numbers, and can be confusing, so make sure to arm yourself with a good map of Venice. Note that *campo* in Venice means square, and in fact all the squares in Venice are called *campo* apart from St Mark's Square or Piazza San Marco, which takes the usual word for square, which is piazza.

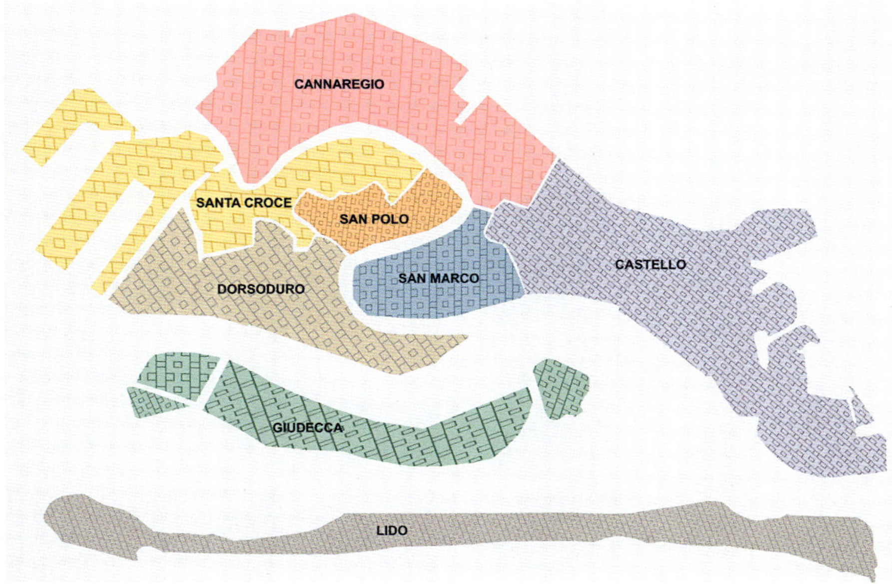

ARRIVING IN VENICE

Most visitors to Venice take the train to the Santa Lucia station, built in 1846 and named after the church that was knocked down to build it. Mary Shelley mentions the building of the railway and says: 'the power, the commerce, the arts of Venice are gone, the bridge will rob it of its romance'.[1] Of course she had a point. Yet as Mark Twain pointed out, it's still

Santa Lucia station and the Church of St Mary of Nazareth. lapas77

a wonderful train journey as you leave the mainland and travel across the narrow strip of land that leads out to Venice.[2] You come out of the station onto the Grand Canal, that stretch of water that has become fixed in the popular imagination with its grand palazzos and all their stories. There she is, right in front of your eyes: Venice. Samuel Rogers shared the poetic stage with the Romantic poets, and in his poem *Italy, a Poem* (1822), he writes about Venice. 'There is a Glorious City in the Sea,/The Sea is in the broad, the narrow streets,/Ebbing and flowing; And the salt sea-weed/ Clings to the marble of her palaces.' The first time you see Venice, she is truly mesmerising. Is there really a city as beautiful as this?

When Mariana Starke wrote *Travels on the Continent: Written for the Use and Particular Information of Travellers* (1820), she effectively wrote one of the first modern guidebooks. Until then travel writing had taken the form of travelogues or descriptions of an individual's travel experiences. Starke described a trip to Venice with her family and gave concrete practical details that could be useful to the modern traveller. She tells us how they

Mariana Starke and the Modern Guidebook

The Po Delta. Lunghammer

slept at the Stella d'Ora in Padua, got up and made the six-and-a-half-hour-journey up the River Po, past the Po Delta and the villas of the River Brenta. In Mestre they hired a gondola to Venice, which took them less than two hours and cost about thirteen pauls, including the *buona mano* or tip. Starke is always practical. When travelling with 'invalids', she suggests an alternative route from Francolino near Ferrara, which takes about twenty hours. Starke knew only too well about such types of travel. Between 1791 and 1798 she travelled around Italy and France with her parents and sister Louisa. Louisa died in 1792 in Nice, while her father died in Pisa in 1794 and is buried in Livorno, known in English as Leghorn at the time.

Once in Venice, Starke gives a list of places to visit.[3] She pays attention to the economics of it all, as she was writing not for rich aristocrats but for families like her own who were travelling on limited budgets. Travel writing, or even writing, wasn't considered to be a respectable occupation for a young lady of her time but Starke did it anyway, albeit anonymously at first. Her first published book was a translation, followed by plays and poetry, and her first travel book was *Letters from Italy, between the years 1792 and 1798* (1800). She continued to write and travel until she was in her sixties and died on 1 April 1838 in Milan.

Lady Sydney Morgan, Nuns and Whores

When Irish writer Lady Sydney Morgan wrote *Italy* (1820), a type of travelogue, she described the country's history in detail and openly sympathised with its desire for unity. Hers was a radical view at the time but then Lady Morgan was radical herself. Her novel *The Wild Irish Girl* (1806) was soaked in nationalism, and it's hardly surprising that she found herself able to identify with the Italian cause for unity and independence. Of Italy's women, she writes, 'The women of all ranks divided into vestals and concubines, were either shut up in convents, or let loose on society free from the duties of maternity and the ties of marriage.'[4] In other words, and according to Lady Morgan, if you didn't get married, you became a nun or a whore. Spot on, Lady Morgan, as these were pretty much the only two options for a lot of women. In each case, you could be autonomous, and in some cases powerful, especially if you became a Mother Superior or a courtesan to powerful men. Lady Morgan comments on the decline of society in comparison to the days of the Venetian Republic. The society of the time revolved around meeting in the houses of rich Venetian aristocratic ladies. The only houses that were still open, she noted, were those of the Countesses Benzon, Michele and Albrizzi, who nevertheless carried forward the talent, beauty and grace of the original daughters and wives of the Venetian Republic.[5]

Sydney, Lady Morgan. Georgios Kollida

4

NORTH OF THE GRAND CANAL

SAN MARCO

Before the train arrived in Venice in the middle of the nineteenth century, visitors arrived by gondola in St Mark's Square. Of course, arriving in Venice by gondola always creates a certain effect. In Sarah Dunant's *In the Company of the Courtesan* (2006), sixteenth-century courtesan Fiammetta and her man servant Bucino arrive in Venice at night to avoid the plague controls. Our heroine Victoria in Charlotte Dacre's novel *Zefloya or The Moor* (1806)

Sunrise in St Mark's Square. Mapics

Saint Mark's Basilica. gammaphotostudio

wants to go off to Venice to see her lover, finds a gondolier and persuades him to give her a lift, all of which was scandalous for the time. In Ann Radcliffe's *The Mysteries of Udolpho* (1794), a popular Gothic novel set in the late sixteenth century, orphan Emily St Aubert leaves war-torn Milan for Verona and then Padua. In Padua they set off along the River Brenta to Venice, past the beautiful villas of the Venetian patricians, where people dance under the trees. They move towards Venice and see its islets and palazzos, the mountains of Friuli in the distance, and St Mark's Square ahead of them, and in this way, they arrive in Venice.

San Marco is the heart of Venice, home to St Mark's Basilica, the Doge's Palace, the Bridge of Sighs, the Piombi prison, and palazzos and cafés where writers over the centuries have gathered. Its original name was Rivoalto until the relics of Saint Mark were brought to Venice from Morocco. Venice didn't have its own patron saint, so in 829 they went to Morocco and got one. Saint Mark, author of one of the four Gospels of the Bible, was one of the most important saints in the Christian world. A basilica was built specifically to contain the body of Saint Mark but then it was burned when the people revolted against the Doge in 976. The body went missing after the fire, but thanks to a miracle it later reappeared. The basilica that we see today is from the eleventh century, with the famous horses riding high above it that were brought back after the conquest of Constantinople. It's also full of pigeons, as Tom Ripley points out in Patricia Highsmith's *The Talented Mr Ripley* (1955) when he comes to Venice and visits St Mark's Square, chooses a restaurant down a side street, and reads the newspaper report that Dickie Greenleaf is missing.

The Grand Canal

Twentieth-century art collector Peggy Guggenheim, in her autobiography *Out of this Century* (1946), republished as *Confessions of an Art Addict* (1960), wrote that: 'If anything can rival Venice in its beauty, it must be its reflection at sunset on the Grand Canal.'[1] It's certainly a remarkable sight; the colours and shapes of the palazzos reflected on the water, punctuated by lights, and all under pink, orange and

gold skies. Indeed Venice, for many of the 20 million people who visit it every year, *is* the Grand Canal or the Canalazzo as the Venetians call it. It's the gondolas, the palazzos, the atmosphere, the romance, the whole

The Grand Canal at sunset. rudi1976

Venetian experience that has inspired writers and painters and musicians and others throughout the centuries.

A lot of the palazzos along the Grand Canal date back to the fourteenth and fifteenth centuries and carry the names of some of the most important families of the Venetian Republic. These were the patrician families of the Golden Book, the official directory of nobles, which contained notes on marital status, births and deaths. Noble lineage was something that the Venetians took very seriously to preserve their class of patrician rulers. Venetian doges were elected. You didn't inherit the role from your father – according to the rules of patriarchy, women didn't count – and this is why preserving the class of nobles was so important.

The palazzos we see today remind us of such families, and that the riches of Venice's past trade with the East provided the money to build such palazzos and made Venice the city it is. A palazzo along the Grand Canal gave you one of the best addresses in Venice and was a way to place the money you'd made in full view. After the fall of the Republic, the palazzos were a lot cheaper to rent. As Mrs Prest tells the narrator of Henry James' novella *The Aspern Papers* (1888): 'Dilapidated old palazzos ... are to be had for five shilling a year.'[2] The palazzos may be grand but the people who live in them have nothing, and Miss Bordereau and her niece Miss Tita are both fine examples of this. During the second half of the twentieth century, Violet de Winter in Muriel Spark's novel *Territorial Rights* (1979) still considers herself to be one of the 'stones, if not the pillars, of Venice' living in her late husband's palazzo along the Grand Canal.[3] Her solution, as many did and do, was to live in a small apartment and rent out the rest of it as apartments. Count Brandolini d'Adda, on the other hand, points out in Gill Johnson's

memoir *Love from Venice: A Golden Summer on the Grand Canal* (2024) that every Venetian palazzo with a few years of neglect becomes a fire hazard![4]

St Mark's Square

It's one of the most famous piazzas in the world, considered, possibly by Napoleon, to be the great drawing

St Mark's Square. Augustin Lazaroiu

room of Europe, while Henry James compared it to a theatre lobby during the interval, where people walked and talked without any particular purpose.[5] He also complained about the visitors and you might be inclined to agree today in spite of being a visitor yourself, but this still doesn't detract from its sheer beauty. In James' novella, *The Aspern Papers* (1888), our narrator without a name spends his evenings in the 'open-air saloon'[6] of St Mark's Square sitting outside Florian's café and eating ices and watching the world go by. It's tempting to do the same, although be prepared to pay for it. In Daphne du Maurier's short story *Ganymede* (1959), a classics professor has a drink at a café in St Mark's Square on his first night in Venice. He notices

a 15-year-old waiter and falls in love. He sees himself as Zeus and the waiter is Ganymede, after the Greek myth of Zeus and Ganymede, where Zeus falls in love with a boy youth named Ganymede. It's a dark, disturbing tale, part of the collection *The Breaking Point* (1959) that du Maurier wrote when she was coming out of a breakdown.

This is the other side of Venice, which unsettles and unnerves, and it's the perfect setting for du Maurier's tale.

Palazzo Ducale

The fourteenth-century Palazzo Ducale, or Doge's Palace, looks out over the Grand Canal from St Mark's Square.

The Doge's Palace with the Campanile or bell tower. Tomas Marek

There were 120 doges of Venice. The first lived on the mainland in Eraclea near Jesolo, then they moved to Malamocco on the Lido Island and then in 810 the seat of the Doge came to Rivoalto or San Marco. Palazzo Ducale is where the scenes in the courthouse are said to have taken place in Shakespeare's play *Othello* (1622) when

Desdemona's father Brabantio accuses Othello of bewitching her to make her fall in love with him.

Foreigners might have viewed Venice as a city of freedoms during the time of the Republic, yet for Venetians it was very highly controlled. The city was ruled mercilessly by the Council of Ten, a form of policing body that protected the state. It's an ever-present threat in the glassblower Corradino's life in Marina Fiorato's book *The Glassblower of Murano* (2007). Corradino is a glassblower from that island, and because of this he's forbidden to leave Venice as the secrets of glassblowing cannot be taken out of Venice. Spying was encouraged, and boxes were placed outside the Doge's Palace where people could put their letters to inform upon fellow Venetians. If you haven't read it, I shall stop here, but if you want to read about the constant threat from the Council of Ten and how this affected people's lives, this is the book to read!

San Marco, 1, www.palazzoducale. visitmuve.it

Piombi Prison

The Piombi prison was up in the eaves of the Doge's Palace and named after the lead roof that made it freezing cold in winter and boiling hot in summer. This was where political prisoners and enemies of the Republic were sent. On the night between 25 and 26 July 1755

Inside the Piombi prison. Philippe Paternolli

Giacomo Casanova was sent there. The conditions were terrible, and Casanova wasn't told that he had only received a five-year sentence; he was convinced he would spend the rest of his life there. A first attempt to escape failed. Then, at dawn on 1 November 1756, Casanova and a monk named Balbi were able to get on to the roof via a hole they'd made in the roof and get into the Palazzo Ducale. They managed to deceive one of the guards and persuade him to open the door, after which they hid at a friend's house, got a gondola and made their way out of the lagoon. It was a spectacular escape from a place that was renowned for being a place of no escape. The whole event resulted in Casanova's exile from Venice. The exile lasted eighteen years and then in September 1774 he was allowed to return.

San Marco, 1, www.palazzoducale.visitmuve.it

Giacomo Casanova

Giacomo Casanova is one of Venice's most famous sons, the ultimate Venetian gigolo, and a prolific writer.

He wrote about his life in his memoirs, and it's thanks to these books that we know so much not only about him but about Venice at that time.

He was born on 2 April 1725 in the *sestiere* of San Marco in what is now Calle Malipiero, and if you walk down there, you'll see a plaque that commemorates his birth. His parents were both actors. His father died when he was young, and he was then looked after by his grandmother while his mother worked. When he was 9, he was sent to school in Padua. He played with the idea of two careers, the church and the military, and started to study Law at the University of Padua but never finished. His real interests in life were pleasure and sex, and indeed his memoirs contain all the details of his sex life, with both women and men.[7] His writing wasn't restricted to his memoirs. He wrote forty-two books in all, including mathematical treatises, a translation of *The Iliad*, poetry, a satirical pamphlet on the Venetian patriciate and other works, including *The Story of My Flight* (1798) in which he described his escape from the Piombi prisons. He's known for his black cape, his large black hat and white mask. It was the usual men's clothing at the time, but for many of us it's what we associate with Casanova.

Andrei Nekrassov

Bridge of Sighs

Lord Byron gave the Bridge of Sighs its name when he opened Canto Four of his poem *Childe Harold's Pilgrimage* (1812) with the following lines: 'I stood in Venice on the Bridge of Sighs;/A palace and a prison on each hand.' This is the bridge over which prisoners were taken from the New Prisons to the court in the Doge's Palace to receive their sentences, and of course the sighs were those of the prisoners. Would they ever leave? Or would they finish their days in this miserable place? The bridge was built at the beginning of the seventeenth century, and enclosed so that prisoners couldn't escape. James Joyce ridiculed it and called it the Breach of all Size in *Finnegan's Wake* (1939). He was never particularly impressed by Venice, and even though he lived in nearby Trieste for fifteen years, he rarely visited.

Literary Palazzos

Palazzo Mocenigo

Palazzo Mocenigo along the Grand Canal is rich in history. It's a collection of four buildings along the Grand Canal between the Rialto Bridge and St Mark's Square. It was the home of

The Bridge of Sighs. Andrea Aigner

Palazzo Mocenigo Casa Nuova. Guido

Doge Tommaso Mocenigo, who in 1418 welcomed the Duke of Winchester during Henry III of England's reign to the old 'Casa Vecchia', another restructured Medieval palazzo and all part of the same Palazzo Mocenigo. The Mocenigos were one of Venice's most important families. Seven of them became doges, while others had highly prestigious roles as Procurators of the Republic. Henry III of France also stayed here as a guest of Doge Alvise Mocenigo when he visited the Venetian Republic in July 1574 and spent the night with the courtesan Veronica Franco. The Palazzo Mocenigo is now home to a museum of the same name, a study centre for the history of textiles, costume and perfume, and is a great place to explore the fashions of the past. George Gordon Byron, better known as Lord Byron, was its most famous resident, and there's a plaque to commemorate the time he lived there between May 1818 and the end of 1819.

George Gordon, Lord Byron

Just before Christmas 1816 a young man named Lord Byron arrived in Venice. He'd been to Italy during his three-year Grand Tour from 1808 to 1811 but never made it to Venice because of the Napoleonic Wars. By this time Byron was a famous poet, the Romantic equivalent of a rock star with his open shirts and long dark curls. He'd published the first two cantos of *Childe Harold's Pilgrimage* (1812) and was an overnight success. His life was filled with scandal. When he got to Venice in 1816, he'd left behind a disastrous marriage with Annabella Milbanke amidst rumours of violence and sodomy, and further rumours

Lord Byron. Georgios Kollidas

of an incestuous relationship with his half-sister Augusta. His previous public and scandalous affair with the married Lady Caroline Lamb led to her calling him 'mad, bad and dangerous to know', although to be fair she lived a turbulent and scandalous life herself. He left England on the excuse that his physician had recommended the Continent due to his heavy drinking. He had no choice. A conviction of sodomy was punishable by death.

Byron being Byron and a great fan of Napoleon, travelled to Italy in a specially commissioned carriage just like that of Napoleon's, stopping off to see various 'Napoleon' locations on the way. He arrived in Venice, stayed at the Hotel Grande-Bretagne for a while, then found lodgings along a small street in San Marco, where he had an affair with his landlord's wife, and anyone else who took his fancy, both women and men.[8] The attitude towards being gay in Venice at this time was relatively relaxed, and besides Byron was the celebrity English lord and poet. Whenever word got out that he had set off to the Lido for the day, young ladies especially would get into their gondolas for the two-hour ride to get there.[9] Byron was the aristocratic bad boy that everyone wanted to see.

When he came to live in Palazzo Mocenigo in May 1818, he brought his mistress Margherita Cogni, a baker's wife known as *La Fornarina*, the woman-baker. She was beautiful, with dark hair, dark eyes and a wild temperament, and very Venetian. He'd met her during the summer while he was staying at La Mira along the Brenta canal. Naturally Byron continued to have other sexual experiences, they had the usual tempestuous rows, and then Margherita threw herself into the Grand Canal one night and was rescued.

Byron played his role to the full. He lived here in Palazzo Mocenigo with Margherita, his daughter Allegra, fourteen servants, and a fox, wolf, two monkeys, dogs and birds that all lived on the ground floor of the palazzo. At night he would insist that candles were lit throughout the whole palazzo to add to the atmosphere. All this was often accompanied by Margherita complaining loudly and very theatrically about his other women.[10] He went swimming in the Grand Canal, followed by his servant in his gondola with his clothes. He wrote the first two cantos of *Don Juan* (1819) here, part of *Manfred* (1817) and *Ode on Venice* (1819), in which he lamented the fact that the city was sinking. He also wrote *Beppo: A Venetian Story* (1818), in which Beppo goes missing at sea, his wife takes a lover and Beppo then returns. When he left the palazzo after a short but eventful eighteen months, it was to go to Ravenna with his lover Teresa Gamba Guccioli and get involved with the Carbonari revolutionary group. Guccioli was married, not that it mattered as he was cast in the role of her *cavalier servente*. This tradition among nobles meant that he was her courtier and had permission to accompany her out in public, to the theatre and to various other social events. Naturally it gave plenty of opportunity for affairs on the side. Not that the husbands always minded. They were often busy with their courtesan of the moment or *cavalier servente* to another lady. It was a system capable of keeping everyone happy.

Venice and the Romantic Poets

Venice provided fertile material for the minds of the Romantic poets, with its crumbling palazzos, some of which now remained empty after the fall of the Republic. William Wordsworth never visited Venice but wrote *On the Extinction of the Venetian Republic* in 1807. Byron published the first part of his poem *Childe Harold's Pilgrimage* in 1812, and the second part in 1818 while he was living in Venice. It's the story of young nobleman Harold, who travels around the world and in the fourth canto goes to Italy and Venice. Samuel Rogers published *Italy, a poem* in 1822, with illustrations by the brilliant painter-of-the-time William Turner to match. All this fired the public imagination and made people want to visit Venice.

Percy Bysshe Shelley

Shelley went to Venice in 1818 as part of negotiations between Byron and Claire Clairmont over their daughter Allegra. Claire was Mary Shelley's stepsister, and the three of them had set off from England to take Allegra to Byron. Allegra was then taken on to Byron in Venice by the maid, and then in August 1818 Percy arrived in Venice to try to gain some kind of access for Claire to see her daughter. He also saw it as an opportunity to renew the acquaintance that he and Byron had made on Lake Geneva when they had

William Wordsworth. wowinside

Percy Bysshe Shelley. Nickolae

taken laudanum and Mary Shelley had the idea for *Frankenstein* (1818), an acquaintance he knew Byron dictated because of his status. It was after his stay with Byron in Venice that Shelley wrote his poem *Julian and Maddalo: A Conversation* (1824). He writes of how Julian and Maddalo spent time riding together on the beach at Lido Island and at Lord Maddalo's palazzo, all of which was inspired by his visit to Byron. Shelley never returned to Venice. He died off the coast of Lerici in 1822, six years later.

Claire Clairmont and Allegra

Claire Clairmont managed to spend some time with her daughter Allegra after Shelley's interventions, but then in November 1818 she was forced to give her back. She tried to see Allegra again, but in March 1821 Byron sent Allegra to a convent in Bagnacavallo, where she died a year later, aged 5. Many years later, writer Daisy Hay was researching her book *Young Romantics: The Shelleys, Byron and other Tangled Lives* (2010) when she found three pages of a manuscript in a New York public library. It was part of a memoir written by Claire Clairmont in her seventies. Clairmont was furious with Byron and Shelley. 'Under the influence of the doctrine and belief of free love, I saw the first two poets of England ... become monsters.'[11]

Mary Shelley

When Mary Shelley first visited Venice in 1818 her life was marked by tragedy. When Percy Bysshe Shelley first went off to Venice, Mary stayed behind to look after the children. Her own baby, Clara, became ill with dysentery, and by the time she arrived in Venice with her, it was too late. Clara died in her arms while Shelley was looking for a doctor.[12]

Mary Shelley is known as the author of *Frankenstein* (1818). What you might not know is that she also wrote two travel books. Her first was *History of a Six Weeks' Tour, through a part of France, Switzerland and Germany, and Holland: with Letters Descriptive of a Sail round the Lake of Geneva, and the Glaciers of Chamouni* (1817). It describes her travels in 1814 when she eloped

Mary Shelley. Lz

at the age of 16 with Shelley and her stepsister Claire Clairmont.

Mary returned to Italy in 1840 with her 23-year-old son Percy and some of his friends, and wrote *Rambles in Germany and Italy in 1840, 1842 and 1843* (1844). Italy was where she had lost her daughter Clara in Venice in September 1818, her son William in June 1819 in Rome, and in July 1822 her husband Percy died in a storm off the coast of Lerici in Liguria. So all three died within the space of four years.

Michelle Lovric

Writer Michelle Lovric spends her time between London and Venice and has written various historical novels, which are often set in Venice. *Carnevale* (2015) tells the story of protagonist Cecilia, who has an affair with Casanova while she is young. Twenty-five years later, she meets Lord Byron, and they too have a relationship. Lovric has also written *The Floating Book* (2003) about the beginning of the printing presses in fifteenth-century Venice. *The Wishing Bones* (2019), *The Water's Daughter* (2020) and *The Undrowned Child* (2009) are all children's books set in Venice.

Couple in Carnival dress in St Mark's Square. pitrs

Alathea Howard, Countess of Arundel

Alathea Howard, daughter of the Earl of Shrewsbury and Mary Cavendish, was also goddaughter to Elizabeth I, and the granddaughter of Bess of Hardwick. Hardwick was a friend of Elizabeth I and a formidable woman herself. At the age of 21, Alathea married Thomas Talbot, Earl of Arundel, in 1606. Elizabeth I had been dead for three years, James I was now on the throne and in 1613 the couple set off on a one-year tour of Italy. The architect Inigo Jones, of whom the Earl was patron, was also with them. Their task was to accompany Elizabeth Stuart, daughter of King James I, to Heidelberg for her marriage to Frederick V, after which they headed off to Italy. They arrived in Venice to banquets and other receptions. In some ways theirs was one of the first Grand Tours, those artistic and cultural tours taken by aristocrats, although it would be another sixty years before Richard Lassels would first use the term, in his book *The Voyage of Italy* (1790). Both Alathea and her husband were art collectors, and so this was another reason for their visit.

In 1620 the countess went back to Italy with her sons. She left them safely at a villa outside Venice and went on to Palazzo Mocenigo, where she made her home. The next summer, the countess found herself at the centre of a scandal that engulfed the entire Venetian Republic. Antonio Foscarini, a Senator of Venice, had been accused of sharing secrets with foreign ministers and receiving money from them, and was strangled the very same night. More so, it was all said to have taken place at Lady Arundel's house, Palazzo Mocenigo. Understandably, this all proved rather stressful for Henry Wotton, Ambassador to Venice. Wotton wrote to her, told her that she would be banished from the Republic, and that she should leave Venice in haste. Lady Arundel wasn't having any of it. She was Bess of Hardwick's daughter, after all. The next morning, she set off to meet the Doge, ensured her continued welcome and got herself invited to the Wedding of the Sea in a state barge. Gifts were sent to her home. When she left six months later with a trail of horses carrying goods, she was exempt from customs. Later in life she became one of the first published women scientists with her work *Natura Extenterata* (1655), a study of herbs and their medical properties.

Lady Mary Wortley Montagu

In 1756, when writer Lady Mary Wortley Montagu was 58, she left her husband in England and moved to Venice. Why she did so is not exactly clear. Her son was grown up, it was all amicable enough, and so off she went to live in Venice. Lady Montagu is famous for her letters, and knew she had talent. They are witty and observant with brilliant descriptions and provide a fascinating insight into

Venetian society at the time. She was also extremely honest, to the point of losing friends and turning people against her. On the other hand, she was on excellent terms with the Venetian noblewomen, paid and received visits, and was given one of the best seats reserved for Venetian nobility when she attended a Mass celebrated by the Doge Francesco Loredan. She writes about the habit of wearing masks to the theatres and in the streets. Everyone who was anyone who came from England came to pay their respects to Lady Montagu, and in this she is typically scathing. She wrote to Lady Pomfret that she couldn't wait to hear 'good sense pronounced in my native tongue'[13] as she'd only heard English spoken by boys and governors for the past five months. As far as she could see, all they were there to do was buy new clothes and sit in some 'obscure coffee-house, where they are sure of only meeting one another'.[14] At times she was capable of being entirely inappropriate, and we know that some of her letters were destroyed because of the nature of their content. Similarly, two of her diaries were destroyed by one of her sisters and her daughter Lady Bute.

Palazzo Barbaro a San Vidal is the cream-coloured palazzo in the middle. jim

Palazzo Barbaro a San Vidal and the Gilded Age

Facing out on to the Grand Canal near the Accademia bridge, this early fourteenth-century Palazzo Barbaro was owned by the Barbaro family. It has two palazzos, one Gothic and one Baroque. The Barbaros were one of the oldest patrician families in Venice and included Francesco Barbaro, one of the most important Venetian humanists and scholars of the fifteenth century,

who also translated ancient Greek texts. When the Venetian Republic fell in 1787, the palazzo was sold off and emptied of its treasures. Towards the end of the nineteenth century the building was bought by Americans Ariana and Daniel Curtis, and it became a focal point for the American and British expat community in Venice. American writers Henry James and Edith Wharton both stayed here. It was a time known as the Gilded Age, which lasted from the

1870s until the 1890s and was defined by its fabulously wealthy families and an emphasis on materialism, all of which contrasted with a deep-rooted inequality within society.

San Marco, 2840 Fondamenta Barbaro

The Curtises at Palazzo Barbaro

American lawyer and banker Daniel Curtis and his wife Ariana came to Venice in 1881 after he had broken a man's nose in a quarrel in a streetcar. The man turned out to be a judge, Curtis spent a night in prison, was then taken to court, and shortly afterwards made the decision he had been thinking of making. He left with Ariana for Venice and a different life. He came across Palazzo Barbaro, rented it at first and then bought it and restored it in 1885.

Palazzo Barbaro became a centre for the American and British community in Venice, a nineteenth-century expat version of the original salons held by eighteenth-century Venetian noblewomen who brought together writers, artists, musicians and intellectuals of the day. Art collector Isabella Stewart Gardner and her husband John (or Jack as he was known) rented part of the palazzo every other summer. Henry James was a guest, as was poet John Addington Symonds, novelist Edith Wharton and the historian Horatio Brown, who was

a specialist in the history of Venice and Italy. James originally introduced French poet and novelist Paul Bourget to the Curtises, along with English writer Violet Paget, who wrote under the pen name of Vernon Lee. James had introduced Isabella Stewart Gardner and Lee in London, and in Venice they became great friends due to a mutual interest in art.

John Singer Sargent also visited and painted the Curtises with their son Ralph and daughter-in-law Lisa. He called it *An Interior in Venice* (1899), a painting that perfectly sums up the social milieu of the time. As it turned out, Mrs Curtis wasn't impressed by the painting as she thought it made her look old. Anders Zorn, another painter friend, painted Isabella Stewart Gardner flinging open the windows of Palazzo Barbaro. She's wearing a white dress and the long string of pearls that she often wore. It captures a moment of an evening when there were fireworks, and she's telling her guests to come and look. Katharine de Kay Bronson was also a regular visitor. She lived at the Palazzo Michiel Alvisi, another place where they all spent time.

Henry James' Venice

American novelist Henry James first arrived in Venice in summer 1869. By this time, James had lived in London for twenty years and had just published his novel *The Princess Casamassima*

Henry James. Morphart

(1886). He went to Venice with a copy of John Ruskin's *The Stones of Venice* (1851). Most people did, as Ruskin was considered the authority on Venice with his three-volume guide to architecture and art. James' first visit signified the start of his long-lasting relationship with Venice over a period of roughly forty years between 1869 and 1907. He stayed with the Curtises at Palazzo Barbaro on many occasions. He liked staying there, found the Curtises to be entertaining and original, and enjoyed being along the Grand Canal, from where he could then visit the city by gondola.

James used Palazzo Barbaro as the inspiration for Palazzo Leporelli in his novel *The Wings of the Dove* (1902), the palazzo where Milly Theale spends the last weeks of her life. He finished his novel *The Aspern Papers* (1888) here in 1887 and wrote his novella *A London Life* (1888). James also stayed with American art collector Isabella Stewart Gardner at Palazzo Gardner. On one visit there was no spare bed, so she set up one for him in the old library at the top of the house. He thought it was wonderful, lying there looking up at the ceiling!

Edith Wharton's Venice

Edith Wharton stayed at Palazzo Barbaro with the Curtises and became friends with Henry James. She'd met James in Paris in 1887 at a dinner. Wharton was 25, James was in his mid-forties, and she was shy and barely spoke to him. By the time she was in her forties herself, Wharton had become James' equal. Their paths would sometimes cross as they had the same publishers and wrote for the same magazines. Wharton had done well in her career, her books were very popular and at the time they became friends sold more copies than his.[15] She set two novels partially in Venice, *The Glimpses of the Moon* (1922) and *The Children* (1928), and a short story, *A Venetian Night's Entertainment* (1929).

Wharton was born into the rich New York family, the Jones, and travelled around Europe as a girl with her parents. She first went to Venice with her father

in 1880, when his doctors had advised him to return to Europe. They visited Venice with John Ruskin's *The Stones of Venice*,[16] and so we can imagine that she will have known the city well from an architectural and artistic point of view. She also read about Italy extensively. In *Italian Backgrounds* (1905), she gives detailed descriptions of the clothes the ladies wore during the eighteenth century, saying when they went out visiting, they wore the traditional three-cornered hat, a *zendaletto* or short cape over their hair and a black silk *bauto*, the traditional Venetian long cape. The book finishes in the Museo Correr, with

mannequins in traditional eighteenth-century costumes, taken from their world by Napoleon.

Wharton was also very good at describing the international set that lived or spent time in Venice. The cosmopolitan society portrayed in *The Glimpses of the Moon* (1922) 'had inter-married, inter-loved and inter-divorced each other over the whole face of Europe'. It was a crowd she knew well. She was part of this society but presented it with all its flaws, including those of the Curtis family in her short story *The Verdict* (1908). Ralph Curtis was the Curtises' son, and his wife Lisa was furious when she read the story to see her husband portrayed as an unsuccessful painter who gives up his painting career to marry a wealthy widow.

Vernon Lee

It was Henry James who introduced Vernon Lee to Isabella Stewart Gardner in London in 1886. Lee, whose real name was Violet Paget, became a regular visitor to Palazzo Barbaro. She was knowledgeable about Renaissance art, Venetian art and artists and shared many interests with Isabella, who loved to go with her on shopping trips to hunt out rare books.[17] Lee was a subversive figure at the time, androgynous because of her name and the men's clothing she wore. She was openly lesbian, an advocate of aesthetic theory, a feminist, pacifist and had an incredibly wide range of interests. She wrote essays, books and short stories on many different subjects, including ghost stories, art history, psychological treatises, the arts, culture, and feminist and pacific texts. Henry James said to his brother William, that she was 'as dangerous and uncanny as she is intelligent, which is saying a great deal'.[18] Her *Studies of the Eighteenth Century in Italy* (1880) is a masterly work and shows the breadth and depth of her knowledge and learning. Lee set her horror story *A Wicked Voice* (1890) in Venice, and dedicated it to singer Mary Wakefield, who she heard sing at the Palazzo Barbaro. Venice is portrayed as 'exhaling, like some great lily, mysterious influences, which make the brain swim and the heart faint – moral malaria'.[19] Venice, as always, is the perfect setting.

Palazzo Contarini Fasan, House of Desdemona

This fifteenth-century Gothic palazzo is one of the smallest palazzos that overlook the Grand Canal in the Campiello Contarini. It's known as the House of Desdemona, where Desdemona lived in Shakespeare's tragedy *Othello* (1622). Italian actress Eleonora Duse lived here at the turn of the twentieth century. After her marriage to actor Tebaldo Checchi broke down, Duse had a relationship with musician and poet Arrigo Boito, who was also

Othello surprising Desdemona in bed. Juergen

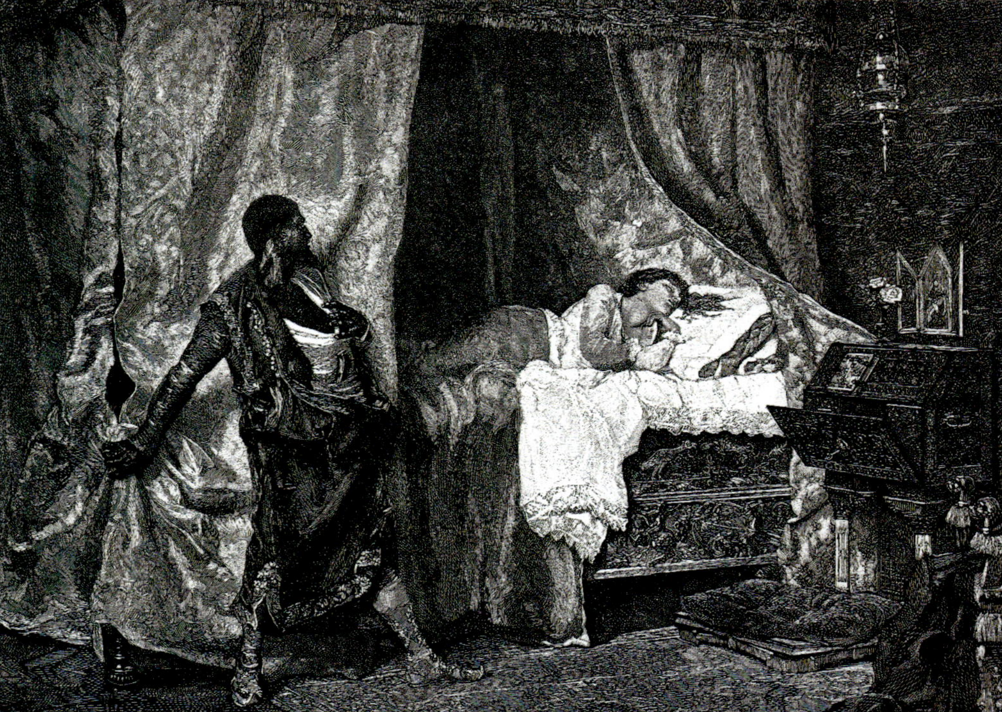

Giuseppe Verdi's librettist and wrote the words for his operas. She then had a nine-year relationship with poet and playwright Gabriele D'Annunzio and acted in some of his most famous roles. Duse was one of the greatest actors of her time and an inspiration to many, including writer James Joyce.

San Marco, 2307 Campiello Contarina

Ca' Giustinian, Once Hotel Europa, and George Eliot

Ca' is the Venetian term for palazzo, and Ca' Giustinian or Palazzo Giustinian faces the Grand Canal along the Calle del Ridotto. It's in the area known as St Mark's Basin, opposite the islands of Giudecca and San Giorgio Maggiore. This fifteenth-century palazzo that was built by the Giustinian family is now home to the Venice Biennale, the international art exhibition that takes place every two years. In 1820 it became the Hotel de l'Europe or the Hotel Europa. French writer Marcel Proust, writer and composer Richard Wagner, and poets Théophile Gautier and Jean Cocteau all stayed here, as did, Edward Lear, who is known for his nonsense poems. Lear was also a respected landscape painter and his nineteenth-century Venice paintings are known for

Palazzo Giustinian. Robert Dering

their evocative atmosphere. Ruskin also stayed here for several weeks in 1876. Yet it's the story of George Eliot and her second husband John Cross that really brings the hotel to life once more.

San Marco, 1364 Calle Ridotto

George Eliot and her Venetian Honeymoon

George Eliot, pen name of Mary Ann Evans, first came to Venice with George Henry Lewes. Lewes was married and unable to get a divorce, so in 1854 they decided to live together anyway and their first trip to Venice was part of an eight-month 'honeymoon' in Europe. At the time Evans had not yet published under the name Eliot; that would come later, in 1858. She hadn't written any fiction yet, but started when Lewes suggested it two years later. It was her first time in Venice, and she was with her beloved Lewes. They spent twenty-five years together, living as husband and wife, although they never married as Lewes was never able to get his divorce. He died on 30 November 1878.

In May 1880 Eliot returned to Venice, and to the Hotel Europa where she had stayed with Lewes. This time she was on a different honeymoon, that of her marriage to John Cross. Cross was twenty years younger than her. One night Cross tried to kill himself by throwing himself off their bedroom balcony and into the Grand Canal.

George Eliot. Morphart

He was rescued and then taken to Verona and back to England. We know very little about all this because Eliot never wrote about it, and it all remains a huge question mark. Why did Lewes try to kill himself? What must Eliot have thought about it all? What was their marriage like? Dinitia Smith, in her novel *The Honeymoon* (2016), researches and recreates it all and imagines what we do not know. She goes back into Eliot's childhood and her life as a young woman and with Lewes to try to make sense of what could possibly have happened. We have the events leading up to Cross's suicide attempt, involving a gondolier named Corradini and a visit to the Rialto area. It's a fascinating read.

Palazzo Giustinian Michiel Alvisi

This rose-pink seventeenth-century palazzo along the Grand Canal has seen writers such as American novelist Henry James and English poet Robert Browning. In the nineteenth century it was still known as Ca' Alvisi, the abbreviated form of *casa* or house used in Venice to refer to the homes and palaces of noble families. Katharine de Kay Bronson moved here in 1875 with her husband Arthur. Both came from wealthy New York families and had the means to set up home here. The Palazzo Michiel Alvisi was attached to the Palazzo Giustinian-Recanati, and this is where Browning and James both stayed. By this time, Browning was a widow and in his sixties. His wife Elizabeth Barrett Browning, who had suffered with ill health for most of her life, had died in Florence in 1861. Browning went back to Venice in 1878 and continued to go every year to stay with the Bronsons. James was in his thirties, never married and never had any relationships with women that were remembered. The first time he came to Venice, he stayed with Bronson, and she later became the inspiration for Mrs Prest in his novella *The Aspern Papers* (1888). Mrs Prest is American and has lived in Venice for fifteen years and is an acquaintance of both the narrator and Juliana Bordereau.

Mrs Bronson was in important figure among the British and Americans in Venice, and was also a patron of the arts. She learned the Venetian dialect so well that she was able to write plays in it. Her home was one of the central meeting points alongside the Curtises home at Palazzo Barbaro. It was a world of meetings in drawing rooms, walks in St Mark's Square, coffees in cafés, and catching up with other American and British friends who either lived in Venice, were visiting or passing through on a journey through Italy. Bronson and Browning became good friends, especially during Browning's later years, and he often brought his sister Sarianna to stay, both in Venice and at Bronson's summer home on the mainland at Asolo, which is incidentally where travel writer Freya Stark made her home. When Browning wrote his collection of poems *Asolando* (1889), it was a reference to those carefree days of random amusement that they shared together. *Asolando* comes from the verb *asolare*, literally to get a breath of fresh air, and he dedicated this collection of poetry to Bronson. Browning and Bronson wrote to each other a lot, and while Browning's side of the correspondence has survived, Bronson's has been lost. Bronson's husband, Arthur, became ill during the 1880s, and went to Paris, where he died a few years later. Browning died on 12 December in Venice at Ca' Rezzonico, the palazzo in Dorsoduro along the Grand Canal that his son, Pen, had only recently bought. His body was returned

to England, and he was buried in Poet's Corner in Westminster Abbey. Bronson died in Florence on 6 February 1901.

Henry James left a testament to his evenings spent at Mrs Bronson's at the end of his essay *Venice* (1882) from his collection *Italian Hours* (1909). It's all in there: the balcony overlooking the Grand Canal, the cigarette, the company, the gondolas, the lights, the serenading, too much serenading, the room behind you that welcomes with more good company and cigarettes. 'If you are wise you will step back there presently,' he ends, and we the reader step back with him.

San Marco, 2207 Calle del Traghetto

The Brownings in Venice

English poet Robert Browning first came to Venice in 1838 when he was 26 to finish *Sordello* (1838), which was set in northern Italy. Set in the thirteenth century, it was about an Italian lyric poet named Sordello da Goito. Browning had worked on it for seven years, but when it was published it was a failure. Later, in 1846, he married poet Elizabeth Barrett. By this time, Elizabeth had already published her collection *The Seraphim* (1838) and *Poems* (1844), both of which gained her widespread recognition. In fact, this is how their courtship began; a case of the meeting of two poetic minds. The perfect marriage? Elizabeth's father

Elizabeth Barrett Browning. Morphart

Robert Browning. Morphart

certainly didn't see it that way, and the couple fled to Italy, firstly to Pisa and then to Florence the year after in April 1847, where they settled at Casa Guidi. It was their home for fourteen years until Elizabeth died from years of ill health in 1861. In May 1851 they went to Venice with their 2-year-old son Pen. Elizabeth loved Venice. 'I have been between heaven and earth since our arrival at Venice … Never had I touched the skirts of so celestial a place.'[20] In her letters, she describes their Venetian life: rides out to the Lido in gondolas, coffee and music in St Mark's Square and a trip to a festa in Chioggia. In 1858 she wrote: 'Give me Venice on water, Paris on land.'[21] Venice always maintained a place in her heart.

Palazzo Fortuny And A.S. Byatt

Palazzo Fortuny, or Palazzo Pesaro Orfei as it was originally known when it was the home of the Pesaro family, is in Campo San Beneto. It belonged to the Pesaro family, but then in 1889 Spaniard Mariano Fortuny y Madrazo began to restore it. He was a painter and clothes designer, born in Granada, who came to Venice with his family towards the end of the nineteenth century to live in the Palazzo Martinengo on the Grand Canal. Fortuny then bought the Palazzo Pesaro Orfei in 1899 so he could be with his lover, Henriette Negrin, a French divorcee of whom his mother disapproved. He opened his fashion house in Venice in 1906.

Campo San Beneto and its Renaissance facades. FredP

A.S. Byatt's book *Peacock and Vine: Fortuny and Morris in Life and at Work* (2016) links Fortuny with the English designer William Morris. Byatt was at the Palazzo Fortuny and each time she closed her eyes she could see what she calls a very English green. The idea developed and she realised that when she thought of Fortuny, she also thought of Morris. She was inspired to learn more about Fortuny from Proust's description of Albertine's Fortuny dress in *A' la recherche du temps perdu* (1913–27), a dress that in Proust's description takes on the features of Venice herself. She was attracted to the fact that both Morris and Proust created their own visual worlds, also through their homes, which reflected and were embodiments of their work. We know that Proust visited Venice in May and October 1900, whereas Byatt visited the Museo Fortuny in Venice during the first part of the twenty-first century. While she was there in the Palazzo Fortuny, she became aware of Morris's ghost. It was this that gave her the idea for the book.[22]

San Marco, 3958

Palazzo Querini Benzon and Marina Querini Benzon's Famous Literary Salon

Palazzo Querini Benzon was the home of Marina Querini Benzon. She was blonde and beautiful, always an advantage at the time, and above all intelligent. She was born in Corfu to a family of nobles in 1757, came to Venice when she married a Venetian in 1777, and started a *salotto* or literary salon. Her *salotto* became known throughout Europe, and was frequented by the sculptor Canova, the Irish writer and poet Thomas Moore, Stendhal. Milanese writer Alessandro Manzoni, whose novel *The Betrothed* (1827) is considered the first great Italian novel, also went there, and of course Byron. It was here that Byron met the married 16-year-old Teresa Guiccioli one night. They began an affair under the guise of the *cavalier servente*, a role that gave Byron official permission to accompany her in public and provided the opportunity for a whole lot of other things. It's also said that Byron had a brief encounter with Benzon, who was 60 at the time. Benzon inspired poet Antonio Lamberti, who wrote the sexually explicit 'La biondina in gondoleta' (the blonde girl in the gondola) about her.[23] The palazzo is situated along the Grand Canal between the Rialto and Accademia bridges.

San Marco, 3927 Calle Benzon

Literary Hotels

Virginia Woolf at the Hotel Casa Petrarca

'There never was such an amusing and beautiful place,' wrote Virginia Woolf of Venice to her friend Violet Dickinson on 4 April 1904.[24] She was on her first visit with her sister Vanessa and her family, and they stayed in the Grand Hotel. Virginia was 22, and she was happy in Venice. In the summer of that same year Violet would nurse Virginia during a suicidal depression. It was the second of at least four depressive episodes, the fourth of which led to her suicide.

Woolf visited Italy seven times during her life, and Venice three times. She came to Venice at the end of her

Virginia Woolf. Wikimedia Commons

honeymoon with Leonard Woolf in 1912. Then in 1932 she returned with Leonard, Roger Fry and his sister Margery on her way to Greece. They left London for Paris, stayed in Paris overnight and then went on to Venice, where they stayed at the Casa Petrarca on the Grand Canal. They then got the boat to Athens via Brindisi on the Sunday. Her diary is rather rushed, a short account of a visit to the island of San Giorgio Maggiore and how 'Venetian light is pale and bright'. She dismisses St Mark's Square and 'that old fraud Ruskin'. She notes a visit that she and Roger Fry make to the Tiepolo church, very probably the Chiesa di Santa Maria del Rosario, also known as the Chiesa dei Gesuiti (Church of the Jesuits) on the Zattera. Rather than focus on the frescoes by Giambattista Tiepolo, she writes 'the thick yellow service with the priests weaving a web in incantation, & the little boys & the reverence & secularity & ancientness made us say This is the magic we want: & magic there must be; so long as magic keeps its place'.[25]

San Marco, 4386, Calle de Le Schiavine

Gritti Palace Hotel

Fourteenth-century Palazzo Pisani Gritti belonged to the Gritti family

Palazzo Pisani Gritti. AlexMastro

and was home to Doge Andrea Gritti during the sixteenth century. Today it's home to the Gritti Palace Hotel. Queen Elizabeth II, Elizabeth Taylor, Brad Pitt, Angelina Jolie, Mick Jagger, Bruce Springsteen and Bob Dylan have all stayed there. During the first part of the nineteenth century it was sold to Baroness Susanna Wetzlar, who rented out rooms. During this time, it became known as Ca' Wetzlar. Then in 1895 it became the Gritti Palace Hotel. Literary guests have included Ernest Hemingway, Graham Greene and W. Somerset Maugham. You can now stay in the Somerset Maugham Royal Suite with its views of the Grand Canal and the island of San Giorgio. Maugham enjoyed staying at the Gritti, where he used to say he felt more like a friend than a guest. Greene also stayed here when in Venice and referred to it as his 'second home'.[26] John and Effie Ruskin rented rooms here when it was Ca' Wetzlar on their extended visit between 1851 and 1852.

San Marco 2467, Campo Santa Maria del Giglio

Hemingway's Venice

Hemingway first came to Italy in June 1918 as a member of the American Red Cross during the First World War. He was 18 years old, wanted to get close to the action, and was soon sent to the front line. On 8 July 1918 he was hit by an Austrian mortar shell in Fossata di Piave in Veneto along the River Piave and taken to the American Red Cross Hospital in Milan. He was lucky to still be alive. While he was there, he fell in love with a nurse, Agnes von Kurowsky, who became Catherine Barkley in his novel *Farewell to Arms* (1929).

Thirty years later, in 1948, Hemingway was on his way to the French Riviera with his fourth wife, Mary Welsh Hemingway. There was a mechanical fault on their ship, and they had to stop in Genoa. Hemingway had been back to Genoa twice as a reporter during the 1920s but had not returned since and had never been back to Veneto. He took the opportunity. This time he was back in Italy as a highly successful author and international celebrity, with novels such as *A Farewell to Arms* (1929), *Death in the Afternoon* (1932) and *For Whom the Bell Tolls* (1940) to his name. They went up to the lakes in Lombardy, to the Dolomites and then across to Veneto. They went to Fossata di Piave, where Hemingway had been injured, and then for the first time he went to Venice. In Venice, they stayed at the Gritti Palace and then moved to the Locanda Cipriani on the island of Torcello. Locanda Cipriani was owned by Giuseppe Cipriani, who also had Harry's Bar where Hemingway went to drink, and the rooms at the *locanda* on Torcello gave him the quiet he needed to write. It was while he was here that he went duck hunting one day with a group of friends. Countess Adriana Ivancich was on the same trip. Hemingway was 49, Ivancich was 18. She became his muse, and it's said that because of her he was able to start writing again after a period of ten years where he had found it difficult. Hemingway's *Across the River and into the Trees* (1950) is based on their relationship. Ivancich was the inspiration for the 18-year-old Countess Renata, who Colonel Cantrell falls in love with. Various locations appear in the book such as Palazzo Gritti, where Cantrell meets Renata, and Harry's Bar in St Mark's Square.

The last time Hemingway stayed at the Gritti Palace was in 1954 for four weeks. It was also the last time he and Ivancich saw each other. Ivancich published a poetry collection, *Ho guardato il Cielo e la Terra* (I have seen the sky and the earth) in 1953. Later, she wrote a memoir about her time with Hemingway, *La Torre Bianca* (1980) – the white tower – in response to Mary Welsh Hemingway's autobiography *How it Was* (1976) about her life with Hemingway. Yet by this time, her mental health and the periods of depression she had struggled with became too much, and in 1983 she committed suicide.

W. Somerset Maugham

Somerset Maugham believed that one of the most pleasant things in life was sitting out on the terrace at the Hotel Gritti with a view of the Basilica della Salute just before sunset. When he said this in 1960 he was already 86 years old. He visited Venice for the last time in 1964, when he was 90, but the visit proved too much for him and didn't go well at all. Maugham had always loved going to Venice, just as he loved travelling and staying in luxury hotels. He often went with his secretary and love of his life, Gerald Haxton, who he had met at the start of the First World War.

Maugham's love of Europe had begun like this. In November 1915 Haxton was found by police in bed with another man in a hotel in Charing Cross in London and charged with gross indecency. At the time sexual relations between men were considered a crime. Haxton, who was American, avoided a prison sentence but was deported several years later. Maugham was married to interior designer Syrie Wellcome at the time and a separation was arranged. Syrie was devastated by the events, and Maugham and Haxton left the country and set off for the south of France. He found Villa La Mauresque at the top of Cap Ferret, and this is where Maugham lived for the rest of his life, and where Winston Churchill, Charlie Chaplin, Picasso, Virginia Woolf and many others came to stay. Each summer he and Haxton would set off around Europe and when they arrived in Italy, they often went to

View of the Grand Canal and Basilica di Santa Maria della Salute. Pawel Pajor

Venice and Florence. After Haxton died of tuberculosis in a private hospital in New York in 1944, Maugham met Alan Searle, who became his secretary and companion in life and in his travels. They were together until Maugham died in 1965 at the age of 91.

Baglioni Hotel Luna

Baglioni Hotel Luna is a short walk away from Piazza San Marco. The building dates from 1118, when it was known as Osteria della Luna and was said to have given hospitality to Templar Knights before they left on their pilgrimages to the Holy Land. Giacomo Casanova and writer and composer Richard Wagner both stayed here, as did Hans Christian Andersen. Andersen wasn't very impressed by

Richard Wagner. Zlatko Guzmic

the city, and didn't stay very long. He called it a 'dead swan floating on water' and complained that it gave him anxiety. In his fairy tale *What the Moon Saw* (1840) an artist becomes friends with the moon and the moon tells him what he has seen. The moon speaks of Venice, where 'On the surface of the ocean a mist often rests, and that is her widow's veil. The bridegroom of the sea is dead, his palace and his city are his mausoleum!'[27]

San Marco, 1243 Calle dell'Ascensione

Nancy Cunard

When British heiress, poet, publisher and political activist Nancy Cunard met black American jazz musician Henry Crowder here at Albergo Luna in 1928 and started an affair, the relationship was scandalous even for the bohemian circles in which Cunard circulated. Her family owned the Cunard Line, which made luxury cruise ships and was worth a fortune. Cunard was the only heir, fell out with her family and was later disinherited by her mother. Yet Cunard defied them all. She was a woman who Samuel Becket praised for her 'spunk and verve'.

Cunard had had relationships with writers such as T.S. Eliot and Ezra Pound, was part of a literary and artistic world, and had just set up her own publishing press known as The Hours Press in a farmhouse in Normandy when she met Crowder. She was already divorced from the war veteran she had married and was in Venice with her lover French poet and writer Louis Aragon. Crowder was in Venice with his band on an eight-week residency. He was married to a seamstress who worked for Eleanor Roosevelt in the White House. During the time Cunard and Crowder spent as a couple, he helped her with her press, and she became very interested in the American Civil Rights movement, helping to publish poetry and work by black writers. However, their time together was both stormy and difficult. Despite it being the longest-lasting

relationship of her life, their affair only lasted for seven years, ending in 1935.

Patricia Highsmith and Venice Hotel Monaco e Grand Canal

When Patricia Highsmith first went to Venice in August 1949, she was accompanied by an Italian banker she'd met the day before in Milan. The man's name was Tonio, and he found a hotel and arranged dinner. She wrote in her diary: 'Tonio most well behaved, never a pass, good hotel. Venice is spectacularly beautiful.'[28] Highsmith doesn't mention that this was the Hotel Monaco e Grand

__Gondola in the Grand Canal.__ Maddalena

Canal on this occasion, but we can imagine she might be here because she mentions that its near St Mark's Square, as is this hotel.

Highsmith loved Venice and had good memories of the Hotel Monaco e Grand Canal, and the 'sunny terrace almost at water level for dining and taking tea'.[29] She writes in her diary about how she returned in 1951 on a trip of Europe that lasted two years. She has drinks with Peggy Guggenheim, who she knows from New York in 1942, and Somerset Maugham, who she finds to be 'short, stutters, extremely polite'.[30] She has coffee in Harry's Bar after a morning shopping trip with Ellen Hill, with whom she had a relationship. The evening consists of cocktails with Peggy Guggenheim again, and then the next day she's at Villa d'Este at Cernobbio on Lake Como. She returned with Ellen in 1953 and again goes for cocktails with Peggy Guggenheim at Harry's Bar, although in 1965 Guggenheim is cool with her and doesn't invite her for cocktails. It's a fascinating insight into Highsmith's life. Her diary entries are short and to the point. For what they do tell us, so much more is left out. What was she thinking when she paired up with a Milanese man named Tonio and went for dinner with him? Why is Peggy Guggenheim cool with her and doesn't invite her for cocktails?

Venice is a place Highsmith returned to, and it became the setting for her novel *Those Who Walk Away* (1967). This cat-and-mouse thriller really plays on the idea of Venice as a maze from which no one can escape. At the beginning, Ray arrives in Venice in the middle of the night and takes a gondola. 'Speechless, white-faced, everyone faced front as if the boat were taking them to their execution.' Even Harry's Bar gets the Highsmith treatment at night: 'Harry's Bar looked like a grey glass-and-stone tomb.'[31] It is perfect Highsmith territory. In *The Talented Mr Ripley*, Tom Ripley is aware that Venice will offer him anonymity and the chance to not be noticed for months. These are psychological thrillers at their very best.

San Marco, 1332-30124 Piazza San Marco

Goethe

German writer Johann Wolfgang von Goethe used to stay in a hotel in San Marco. The hotel is no longer there, but his travel account *Voyage in Italy* (1816) became one of the most famous in European literature. He wrote it after spending almost two years from 1786 to 1787 travelling through the country to places such as Lake Garda, Verona and Venice, after which he went south to Rome, Naples and Sicily. He spent two weeks in Venice in 1786. He enjoyed Venice, loved Rome more, but it was Sicily that was the

Johann Wolfgang von Goethe. Archivist

key to everything he claimed. One could not see Italy without seeing Sicily.

Giustina Renier Michiel and Her Literary Ridotto

'*Prima di tutto sono Venezianissima*' – First of all, I am very Venetian – claimed one of the city's most loyal women, Giustina Renier Michiel. She was born in 1755 into a family that had produced two doges for Venice. Her grandfather, Paolo Renier, was the penultimate doge, while her uncle on her mother's side was Ludovico Manin, the last doge. Giustina belonged to a group of cultured and educated women who were often aristocratic, but not always, and held cultural and literary meetings in their homes. In Italian such a meeting was known as a *ridotto* in eighteenth-century Venice, after the public and private gambling houses that were so prevalent. Giustina held hers at her home in the Corte Contarina in the parish of San Moisè. She welcomed writers such as Byron, Madame de Staël and the Italian writer Ugo Fuscolo, Maria Querini Benzon who held her own successful *salotto* as these meetings were known, and Giustiniana Wynne. Giustina was married to Marcantonio Michiel and had three daughters, one of whom died young. It was an unhappy marriage, and Giustina sought a divorce, which was granted. She was then free to pursue her intellectual pursuits as she pleased. Although Giustina never became the Dogaressa, she was held in very high regard and treated as if she were one. She's most known for *L'Origine delle Feste Veneziane* (The Origin of Venetian Festivals) of 1817, and she also translated some of Shakespeare's plays into Italian.

Literary Cafés and Bars

Venice has a long history of cafés, or coffee houses as they were known. The first coffee beans were brought to Venice at the beginning of the sixteenth century. They were originally sold in the pharmacy and immediately branded the

ver0nicka

'drink of the devil' by various Christians. By the eighteenth century, coffee houses had become popular and in 1750 Venetian playwright Carlo Goldoni wrote a play called *La Bottega del Caffè* (1750), or the coffee shop. It's one of his most famous works and really brings to life the coffee house as a social meeting place and a venue from which to watch the world. The coffees that eighteenth-century Venetians drank were different to those we drink today. The coffee machine hadn't yet been invented, so the beans were boiled and the resulting drink then filtered and served alongside the gossip and scandal of the day. Note that the cafés mentioned below are high end, so you will pay more. All have preserved their eighteenth-century charm, and in Carnival when people are dressed in eighteenth-century costumes, they are a real pleasure to visit.

Caffè Florian

If you could go back to the Venice of the eighteenth century, you might have seen Giacomo Casanova flirting with various women, and Venetian writer and intellectual Gasparo Gozzi or playwright Carlo Goldoni sitting at the tables of the Caffè Florian. Coffee houses were great social levellers, where people of all classes gathered, and nobles sat alongside merchants, ambassadors, and ordinary people. At one point, Casanova was a spy for the Council of Ten when he came back to Venice after his exile, and coffee houses were the perfect places to listen in on other people's conversations and learn what was going on. You went there for the coffee, the gossip and the latest social scandals; and if anyone created scandal it was Casanova.

Caffè Florian was one of the earliest coffee houses in Venice, and is certainly the oldest that is still open today. It was originally opened as *Alla Venezia Trionfante* (To the Triumphant Venice) on 29 December 1720 by Floriano Francesconi, who provided the inspiration for Goldoni's coffee house owner Rodolfo in *La Bottega del Caffè*. It has seen some of the greatest figures of European and American literature sit at its tables. Byron came here at the beginning of the nineteenth century and enjoyed taking his place in the Oriental Room. Alexandre Dumas, writer of *The Count of Monte Cristo* (1844) and *The Three Musketeers* (1844), Charles Dickens and German writer Johann Wolfgang von Goethe all came here, too. Later, the café was a favourite with Marcel Proust, and then in the early nineteenth century Gabriele d'Annunzio and Eleonora Duse, and Ernest Hemingway.

French philosopher and writer Jean-Jacques Rousseau, whose phrase 'Man is born free, and everywhere he is in chains' inspired the French Revolution, also came here, as did French writer, philosopher and political theorist Madame de Staël. She was famous for the novel *Corinne, or Italy* (1807). Set in Italy, and in Venice, it was about an Italian poet named Corinne and her affair with an English lord, and was Teresa de Guccioli's favourite novel. Guccioli was an Italian countess and her lover Byron was an English lord and poet, so it's easy to understand why the story appealed. In the nineteenth century, coffee houses had a political as well as a social role. During the Austrian occupation, Caffè Florian was a meeting place for patriots, and during the 1848 insurrection against the Austrians, it was used as hospital for their wounded.[32] It's also where Carlo takes Julia Garnet for a prosecco in Sally Vickers' *Miss Garnet's Angel* (2000), which is the beginning of an attraction.

Caffè Florian, Piazza San Marco, 57 www.caffeflorian.com

Grancaffè Quadri

The Grancaffè Quadri is the other most famous coffee house in Venice, where you can really enjoy the charm of its surroundings and dream of previous times. Owner Giorgio Quadri opened the doors in 1755. He was from Corfu and had recently arrived

Frozen Action

in Venice. From 1830 it passed under new management and a restaurant was added upstairs. Byron, Stendhal and Marcel Proust all came here.

Grancaffè Quadri, Piazza San Marco, 121
www.alajamo.it

Caffè Lavena

Caffè Lavena started life in 1750 as Regina d'Ungheria, or the queen of Hungary, as a reference to the tradition of the coffee houses in Central Europe. It became Caffè Lavena in 1760 when it was bought by Carlo Lavena. It was a favourite of the Marchesa Luisa Casati, who used to walk through St Mark's Square with her pet cheetahs on diamond leads, and of her lover Gabriele D'Annunzio and his lover before Luisa, Eleonora Duse.

Caffè Lavena, Piazza San Marco, 133/134
www.caffelavena.it

Harry's Bar

Harry's was a favourite haunt of Ernest Hemingway during the middle of the last century. There he would sit at his table, sometimes back from his hunting trip on the island of Torcello, accompanied by a few dead birds.[33] Hemingway first went to Harry's Bar during his first visit to Venice in autumn 1948, and became a regular. It is very different to the historic cafés in St Mark's Square, with its simple décor and wooden tables. It was opened on 13 May 1931 by Giuseppe Cipriani and was the result of a loan. Ten years previously, an American, Harry Pickering, had been in Venice with his aunt, but he had an alcohol problem and fell out with her. He had no money to pay for his ticket home, and so Cipriani had lent him the money. Pickering came back to Italy and paid Cipriani back, and Cipriani was then able to open Harry's Bar with the money. Somerset Maugham, Dorothy Parker, Truman Capote, F. Scott Fitzgerald and Peggy Guggenheim all drank there, while Jan Morris walked in there one day in summer 1945 as a young British officer soon after the end of the Second World War. The people in the bar gave him cold stares, but the people behind the bar were welcoming, and Morris always returned.[34] Go for a Bellini if you can. It's made with prosecco and white peach juice and named after the Venetian painter Giovanni Bellini. When Charles Ryder goes off to Venice with Sebastian Flyte in Evelyn Waugh's *Brideshead Revisited* (1945),

he speaks of the champagne and hot cheese sandwiches at Harry's Bar as a memory to be treasured. Harry's Bar is also where the Italian dish carpaccio was invented by Giuseppe Cipriani in 1950. The story goes that a Venetian countess was ordered by her doctor to eat raw meat. When she went to Harry's Bar and asked for it, the carpaccio was the result.

Harry's Bar, Calle Vallaresso, 1323 www.cipriani.com

The PEN Conference, Venice, 1949

The PEN Group was founded in 1921 in London by English novelist John Galsworthy, and originally stood for Poets, Essayists, Novelists. Later, editors and playwrights were added. Its purpose was to promote friendship and co-operation between writers, and its first congress took place in London in 1923. In September 1949 the congress took place in Venice. Poets W.H. Auden, Stephen Spender and Natasha Spender, Edwin Muir and Willa Muir, and Cecil Day Lewis all took part, and were photographed around the city and sitting outside at the café tables in St Mark's Square.

Marciana Library

The Biblioteca Marciana, or the Marciana national library, is one of Italy's biggest ancient libraries, with more than a million works. The idea for the library began in the fourteenth century when the scholar and poet Francesco Petrarca, also known as Petrarch, who lived in Venice from 1362 to 1367, wanted to dedicate his collection of books to the city. There was nowhere to put them, so he gave them to the city of Padua instead. Nevertheless, the idea for a public library had been sown. Further attempts were made to open a library over the next couple of centuries, and finally in 1603 the Official Public Library of Venice was opened. It is famous for the many texts, manuscripts and books that are held there. One of the highlights is Fra Mauro's map of the world, a fifteenth-century planisphere.

Biblioteca Marciana, Piazza Marco, 7; opening hours Monday to Friday, 8.30am–6.30pm

Marciana Library. rudiernst

Libreria Antiquaria Linea D'Acqua

Linea D'Acqua is Venice's most important antiquarian bookshop, not to be confused with a library. '*Libreria*' in Italian means bookshop, whereas 'biblioteca' is the word for library. It specialises in first editions, antique books, and precious antique engravings such as those by Canaletto, Tiepolo and Marieschi. If you're interested in the world of antique books, this is your place.

Libreria Antiquaria Linea d'Acqua, Calle de la Mandola, 3717D www.lineadacqua.it

Isola Di San Giorgio Maggiore

If you look out into the lagoon from St Mark's Square, you'll see the island of San Giorgio Maggiore with its tenth-century Monastery of San Giorgio. The garden inside the monastery is home to the Borges Labyrinth and is named after twentieth-century Argentinian writer Jorge Luis Borges. It's made up of over three thousand boxwood plants, trimmed in the shape of his surname, Borges. There's also a sensory experience for the visually impaired as Borges had lost his sight completely when he died.

Island of San Giorgio Maggiore. Aliaksandr

Monastery of San Giorgio and Borges Labyrinth. Panama

CANNAREGIO

If Venice is a fish, as Tiziano Scarpa claims at the beginning of his travel guide *Venice is a Fish* (2000), Cannaregio is its dorsal fin. It was home to Venice's Jewish ghetto, where Marco Polo lived and then returned, and was popular with seventeenth-century writers and ambassadors. Cannaregio is also Venice's most popular residential area and has plenty of bars, restaurants, and cafés, great for a coffee or *spritz Veneziano* as you read more stories about writers in Venice. You could also head off for *cicchetti*, the traditional Venetian tapas of slices of bread with various toppings, washed down with a glass of local white wine.

Locals recommend *Bacaro Al Momoleto de Le Voie* (www.bacaroalmomoleto. com) and *Al Timon* (www.altimon.it). Do bear in mind they're in different areas of Cannaregio, so choose one or the other. If you're at home, pour yourself a glass of something nice, prepare a few dishes of nuts and crisps, and read on.

Donna Leon

American-born writer Donna Leon first came to Venice in the 1960s to accompany a friend who was going to study painting there. It wasn't the accepted thing for young women to go off to Italy alone, and so Leon was

Cannaregio with the Tre Archi bridge. Alex Zosimov

invited to go, too. She loved Venice and remembered thinking at the time that this was the place she wanted to be.[35] She then went off around the world to teach English, and then in 1981 when she decided it was time to settle down, she returned to Venice. She had friends there. She started to write in Venice, and her first novel *Death at La Fenice*, was published in 1992. In it she introduced her readers to the detective Commissario Guido Brunetti and a Venetian world of suspense where a world-famous conductor at La Fenice theatre has died. Leon has now written thirty-three books in the internationally bestselling series. She's also written

My Venice: and Other Essays (2013), a collection of more than fifty essays that cover Venetian topics such as refuse, diplomatic incidents and the Italian man. If you want to go visit the theatre, you'll find it in San Marco in Campo San Fantin.

Corte Seconda Milion and Marco Polo

Venice was a city of travellers and explorers, and the most famous of these is Marco Polo. Polo was born in 1254 here in the *sestiere* of Cannaregio and lived in the Corte Seconda del Milion with his family. His father and uncle were both wealthy merchants, and at the age of 15 Marco went off

Marco Polo. Chivery

to China with them. He stayed in Asia for around twenty-five years and was highly respected by the emperor Kublai Khan. When he finally came back home again, there were great celebrations, but no one believed the stories he told. He spent a year in prison when he was taken by the Genoese while he was fighting against them with his fellow Venetians. While he was there, he met a Tuscan writer and it was this that inspired him to write down all his stories. It resulted in his book *Il Milione*, which was effectively one of the first travel books although at the time no one believed the stories it contained!

Thomas Coryat, Who Walked from Somerset to Venice and Wrote About it

Thomas Coryat, or Coryate as he's also known, was the son of rector George Coryat, and born in Odcombe in Somerset, probably in 1577. He went to Oxford University, left without a degree, and in 1603 he entered the court of Prince Henry Prince of Wales, eldest son of King James VI of England and I of Scotland. At court he was officially an entertainer, although he was probably more of a jester.[36] Coryat's father, George, died in 1607, and it was then that the idea of his journey and book came to him. He would walk to Venice and then write about it. He had two reasons: it would make him money and it would make

Reproduction of a sixteenth-century map of Europe. Malgorzata Kistryn

him famous, and in his book he'd also give advice to future travellers.[37] On 14 May 1608 Coryat set off to Dover and began his six-week journey via France and through northern Italy to Venice, give or take a few lifts that he could get on the way. It wasn't the type of thing people did. People had travelled across Europe for pilgrimages, wars and diplomatic missions, but the Grand Tour as a cultural rite of passage for young aristocrats wouldn't take off for another century. Walk across Europe? Coryat was viewed as very strange indeed.

Coryat's Crudities

Coryat reached Venice on 28 June 1608, six weeks after he'd set off, and as promised he wrote about it all. He disapproved of the courtesans with their breasts on display, was equally shocked by the women who played female parts at the theatre and highly surprised that theatre seats were reserved for the best courtesans. He also noted a type of high platform clogs or pattens known as *calcagnetti* that were worn by patrician Venetian women and courtesans. They were often as high as 60cm, so that the help of a servant was required for them to walk and protect their dresses from mud, and Coryat had little sympathy when he saw one woman fall. Coryat stayed in Cannaregio with other Englishmen,[38] near the house of English Ambassador Henry Wotton, who Coryat visited. He visited the markets, commented how well stocked they were, and was particularly attracted by the red, yellow and green melons, 'but the red is the most toothsome of all'.[39] His description of the fork is the first published in the English language, and he brought some

back from Italy. As it turned out, people were slow to adopt them as they were quite happy using a spoon, knife and their hands.

Coryat went back home and in 1611 he published his book, the same year as the King James Bible was published, and dedicated it to Prince Henry. Its full title was: *Coryat's Crudities: hastily gobled up in five moneths travells in France, Savoy, Italy, Rhetia commonly called the Grisons country, Helvetia alias Switzerland, some parts of High Germany and the Netherlands, newly digested in the hungry air of Odcombe in the County of Somerset & now dispersed to the nourishment of the travelling members of this Kingdom.* Playwright Ben Jonson, the poet John Donne and painter and architect Inigo Jones were also at court, and both Donne and Jones offered mock heroic verses, while Jonson edited it and wrote the introduction. It was one of the first travel books printed in English, although when it came out Coryat was openly ridiculed. There were many who still couldn't understand why on earth he had wanted to walk to Venice in the first place. We can only be glad that he did. It's a fascinating read and a valuable record of Venice at the beginning of the seventeenth century.

Tim Moore retraces Coryat's journey in an old pink Rolls-Royce in his book *Continental Drifter: Taking the Low Road with the First Grand Tourist* (2001).

Coryat's Crudities.

Courtesans

It was Catholic priest Richard Lassels in his book *The Voyage of Italy* (1670) who first warned men on their Grand Tours against the dangers of the courtesans and prostitutes in Venice. You could pick up diseases that could then make you sterile, he told them, which was probably not a desirable outcome if you needed to father an heir. Thomas Coryat was also critical of the courtesans and the position they held within society. He noted how the gentlemen of the city indulged but kept their wives at home. Coryat was right. Venetian patrician wives lived very sheltered lives at home and, while Venice was portrayed as a city of freedoms, this didn't include women. While Coryat was there, he visited one of the most important courtesans of the time, and provided a description of the palazzo and the lady herself. What happened while he was there? Coryat insisted it was all innocent. He claimed that Venice had 20,000 courtesans at the time, many 'so loose that they are said to open their quivers to every arrow'.[40] We know that at the end of the sixteenth

ChiccoDodiFC

century, Venice certainly boasted 12,000 courtesans and prostitutes out of a population of 130,000. The city had an official register, the *Tariffe delle Puttane di Venezia*, which detailed addresses, tariffs and what each woman excelled in. The courtesans had a specific role within Venetian society. The Republic was concerned about the number of gay men, and allowing courtesans and prostitutes was seen as a deterrent. Venetian families, those of the famous Golden Book with details of patrician families, couldn't always afford to marry off all their children. They used their wealth to provide huge dowries for the few. Surplus daughters filled the nunneries, often a preferable option to being married off to someone you didn't like, while the surplus men provided custom for the courtesans. There were two types of courtesans at the time. The *cortigiana onesta* was cultured and had many rich and powerful men amongst her clients, while the *cortigiana di lume* or prostitute of the light, worked in the Rialto area and lit candles at her windows. The latter are the ones that Coryat will have seen standing out in the streets or up on the windows, with their breasts on full display.

In the Company of the Courtesan – Sarah Dunant

Sarah Dunant's *In the Company of the Courtesan* (2006) charts the journey of Fiammetta Bianchini through the eyes of her man servant, Bucino. In Rome Fiammetta enjoys the status of being a cardinal's courtesan. However, during the Sack of Rome in 1527, Fiammetta and Bucino are forced to flee. They make the journey up to Venice, where Fiammetta is originally from, and start again. When Bucino jokes that Fiammetta would make a 'ravishing enough nun for a while',[41] he is pointing to the reality that many women faced. Convents served the basic purpose of giving shelter and food, far preferable to starving on the streets. When they arrive in Venice, their goal is to establish Fiammetta as a courtesan with her own palazzo and rich and powerful clients, as it's this that gives her the status of courtesan. If you want to find out more about the life of courtesans in Venice, this is the book to read.

The Jewish Ghetto

'Ghetto' comes from the Venetian word *ghèto* or *foundry*, which comes from the verb *gettare* or to cast. The reason for this is that the Jewish ghetto in Venice was built on what was once a foundry. It is the oldest in Europe and was established in 1516. Thomas Coryat first

Campo del Ghetto Nuovo. bortnikau

referred to the 'ghetto' in his *Crudities*, making it the first recorded use of the word in English. At the time Jews were only allowed to attend one university in the Venetian Republic, that in Padua. For a handful of intellectuals who lived in the ghetto, a lively cultural and intellectual life started to take shape.[42] The ghetto was abolished by Napoleon in 1797 when he entered Venice and set fire to its gates.

Sarra Copia Sullam

Sarra Copia Sullam was a writer and poet who was born in the Jewish ghetto into a wealthy family around 1592.

When she was born, Barbara Strozzi, Elena Cassandra Tarabotti and Veronica Franco had all written and published works. Moderata Fonte had written *The Merits of Women*, considered one of the great early feminist texts, and published posthumously in 1600 by her 15-year-old daughter, when Sullam was around 8 years old.

Around 1613, Sarra married Giacobbe Sullam, and she knew Leon Modena, the Jewish scholar who also lived in the Venetian ghetto. Around 1618 she set up her literary salon, and for the next six years it was a lively cultural meeting place, which attracted both Christians and Jews. Meetings took place during the day because the gates were locked at night. Poet and bishop Baldassare Bonifaccio also frequented her salon and was a member of the academy that had formed there. He attacked Sullam in his *On the Immortality of the Soul: A Discourse* (1621). Sullam's response, *Manifesto* (1621), was her first published work. Sulam closed her salon in 1624, and we know nothing about her life after this. She died on 15 February 1641.

Moderata Fonte and the Merits of Women

Sixteenth-century writer Moderata Fonte was born in 1555 as Modesta del Pozzo. Both her parents died when she was only a year old and she was sent to a convent to be educated, where they noted that she had a good memory. When Moderata was 17, she married lawyer Filippo de Zorzi and had four children, but she always continued to write and produce poetry. *The Merits of Women* (1600) was her most significant work and draws upon a tradition that started with Christine de Pizan, who had been born in Venice but moved to France with her family when she was only 4 years old. Pizan had written *The City of Ladies* in French, which was published in 1405. Pizan's book was a defence

of women that contrasted with the attitude of many men at the time. She praised women and celebrated their virtues. Fonte's book presented the same themes as a conversation in a garden between seven women. It was published posthumously in 1600 by her 15-year-old eldest daughter, Cecilia.

Moderata Fonte's Il Merito delle Donne *(The Merits of Women).*

Chiesa di San Marcuola and Caterina Dolfin

Poet Caterina Dolfin was buried here alongside her mother in the Chiesa di San Marcuola. She was born in Venice in 1736, and when her father died, she was married in 1755 at the age of 19. This is when Dolfin started to write poetry, and it's been suggested that she did this as a way of coping with the marriage. It was around this time that she met Andrea Tron, who introduced her to various intellectuals and nobles. Dolfin decided to challenge her marriage and claimed that it was illegal because it had taken place against her will. In 1767 in Padua and then in 1768 in Venice, she published her most famous collection of poems, a collection of sonnets inspired by her father. The marriage was finally annulled in 1772. Her home was raided in the same year, and she was found to have books by French writers such as Rousseau, Voltaire and other writers of the French Enlightenment who were seen as a threat to the status quo.

Dolfin married Tron in 1772, and he then became Procuratore of Venice, the second most important position after Doge. Caterina then welcomed intellectuals and writers at their official residence. While Tron was the Procuratore of Venice, Caterina had become the *procuratessa*, but in 1774 this period came to an end. Caterina continued to hold cultural meetings at her home until her death in 1793.

Cannaregio, 1762 Campiello de la Chiesa

Shakespeare's Venice

When Coryat set off on his walk to Venice in 1608, he was visiting a destination that English theatregoers were aware of. William Shakespeare had

The Chiesa di San Marcuola, where Caterina Dolfin is buried. Matteo Pasotto

recently referred to Venice in several of his plays and used it as a setting for *The Merchant of Venice* (1600) and *Othello, the Moor of Venice* (1604). Did Shakespeare ever visit Venice? Some say certainly not, others have suggested he must have had first-hand knowledge to write the way he did. Both Shylock and Othello are outsider figures in Shakespeare's plays, as this will have been how they were viewed at the time. Shylock is a Jew and Othello is a moor. At the time, Venice was a meeting point for many cultures, and so Venice was the perfect setting for Shakespeare to explore such themes. There is no mention of the Jewish quarter in *The Merchant of Venice* (1600), although Shylock has become the most famous Jewish character in English literature

and it's easy enough to imagine him having lived there among the other moneylenders in the ghetto. *Othello* is said to have come from the Italian play *Hecatommithi* (1565), which begins with the sentence 'There was a moor in Venice.' Did Shakespeare speak Italian? It's quite possible that he did, as plays that he used as sources were very often only available in Italian.[43]

John Milton

Poet John Milton, most famous for his work *Paradise Lost* (1667), was a younger contemporary of Shakespeare's. We know that he spent time in Venice as in April and May 1639 he arranged for books to be shipped back to his home in England from here. He was out there on his own Grand Tour of France, Italy and Switzerland.[44]

William Shakespeare. Claudio Divizia

John Milton. wowinside

Living the Venetian Dream

If you want to find out more about people who have made their homes in Venice and written about it, here's a selection of books to try:

Philip Gwynne Jones, To Venice with Love: *A Midlife Adventure*, Constable (2019)
Philip Gwynne Jones is the author of the Nathan Sunderland thrillers. This is the story of how he and his wife Caroline moved from Edinburgh to Venice in 2011.

Polly Coles, *The Politics of Washing: Real Life in Venice*, The Crowood Press (2013)
Polly Coles moves to Venice with her Venetian husband and children for a year. It's a refreshing look at day-to-day life in Venice, far from the Venetian dreams and the stereotypes.

Marlena de Blasi, *A Thousand Days in Venice*, Virago Press Limited (2003)
Cook and journalist Marlena de Blasi moves to Venice and falls in love with a Venetian bank manager. Several months later, she marries

Ekaterina Belova

him. The book is filled with plenty of food and recipes.

Marie Ohanesian Nardin, *Beneath the Lion's Wings*, Waterline Publishing (2018)
A thirty-something woman goes to Venice and falls in love with a gondolier. Marie herself is married to her own gondolier and has lived in the Venetian countryside since 1987. The lion's wings of the title are those of the bronze lion in St Mark's Square, the symbol of St Mark, the patron saint of Venice.

ChantalS

CASTELLO

Castello is Venice's most eastern district and includes the island of San Michele, where you'll find the city's cemetery. The city's *Arsenale* or Arsenal is in Castello, recognisable by the two towers at its entrance. It was the world's most famous shipyard, symbol of the power and riches of the Venetian Republic, and at one point 16,000 people are said to have worked there. Dante Alighieri referred to it at the beginning of Canto 21 of *Inferno* (hell), the first of his three-part masterpiece *The Divine Comedy* (1321), and you can see a bust of Dante on the right of the main entrance. The Arsenale is now part of the Venice Biennale, and hosts exhibitions and various art instalments. Castello also includes the island of St Elena, which is at the far east of the district and linked by five bridges. St Elena is a relatively quiet area of Venice with the city's biggest park, the Parco delle Remembranze. It's the perfect place to go if you're wanting a quieter morning or afternoon to do a bit of

The district of Castello. Katvic

Entrance to the Arsenale. Gur

reading. It's thought that Marco Polo was buried in the family tomb here in the church of San Lorenzo in Campo San Lorenzo, although the tomb has been lost.

Arsenale, Campo de la Tana, 2169, check opening hours before you visit

Riva Degli Schiavoni

The Riva degli Schiavoni is the grand waterfront stretching along St Mark's Basin from St Mark's Square. It's characterised by the monuments and palazzos that you can find along it such as the Chiesa della Pietà, the church associated with Vivaldi, and the Palazzo Due Torri (Palazzo of the Two Towers), where Petrarch or Francesco Petrarca lived. A walk along here is a must, and especially at sunset. To get an idea of what this area looked like in the first half of the seventeenth century, look up Canaletto's painting *Venice: the Riva degli Schiavoni* (1740–45). Henry James

Riva degli Schiavoni. BiankaB

also stayed along here at number 4161, when he first came to Venice in 1869, while Giacomo Casanova fled to Palazzo Brigadin on the night he escaped from the Piombi prison. His friend, Matteo Brigadin, took him in and gave him the money and necessary documents to flee Venice.

Hotel Danieli

The Hotel Danieli, with its view over the lagoon towards the Basilica di Santa Maria della Salute, is at the end of the Grand Canal along the Riva degli Schiavoni, opposite the island of San Giorgio Maggiore. Part of the hotel we see today was once the fourteenth-century Palazzo Dandolo. The Dandolo family was one of the most powerful in Venice. Enrico Dandolo was the first of the four doges belonging to the family, and it was he who conquered Constantinople in 1204 and brought back the four Horses of St Mark that stand above the Great Archway up on St Mark's Basilica. The palazzo became the Hotel Danieli in 1822. German writer Johann Wolfgang von Goethe, Byron, French writers Honoré

Gabriele D'Annunzio. nickolae

de Balzac and Marcel Proust, and Charles Dickens all stayed here. It's also where George Sand arrived with her lover Alfred Musset in the winter of 1833. Actress Eleonora Duse and poet Gabriele d'Annunzio spent their first night together here on 25 September 1895. He was the poet and she was his muse and one of the greatest actors of her time.

Riva degli Schiavoni, 4196, www.hoteldanieli.com

Ruskin's Venice

The book to read before any trip to Venice was the three-volume *The Stones of Venice* (1851–53) by John Ruskin. Ruskin first went to Venice in 1835 when he was 16. He went back again in

1841 and 1845, and when he married Euphemia (Effie) Gray, as she was known, the couple spent part of their honeymoon there between 1849 and 1850. Ruskin was 29, while Effie was only 19. They stayed here at the Hotel Danieli. By this point Ruskin had written two books, *Modern Painters* (1843) and *The Seven Lamps of Architecture* (1849), both of which had been well received. They returned in 1851–52 and rented rooms at Palazzo Gritti, where Ruskin wrote the second volume of *The Stones of Venice*. Effie was very enthusiastic about Venice. She didn't mind being left alone all day while Ruskin occupied himself with his work. If anything, she enjoyed the

John Ruskin. wowinside

freedom it gave her. Yet it was a difficult marriage from the start. Effie was lively and outgoing and gathered admirers; the marriage didn't last and caused a society scandal.[45] Effie had fallen in love with the painter John Everett Millais, a friend and protégé of Ruskin's. She asked for her marriage to Ruskin to be annulled as it had never been consummated, and a year later Effie and Millais got married.

Ruskin never remarried and returned to Venice on various occasions. The last time was in 1888, and by this time it was evident he wasn't well. He suffered from periods of madness, what we now know as encephalopathy or brain dysfunction. In the latter years of his life, he retreated to his home in Cumbria, saw very few people, and died in 1900 at the age of 80. His book *The Stones of Venice* was published in three volumes between 1851 and 1853 and remains a classic text on Venice. Effie found her happiness with Millais, and they had eight children. She died in 1897, a year after Millais.

George Sand in Venice

On 31 December 1834 a French couple arrived in Venice. She was Amantine Lucile Aurore Dupin, better known to all as George Sand, independent, unconventional, liberated, in many ways an early feminist who dressed in men's clothes and smoked cigars as she pleased. He was Alfred de Musset, poet,

George Sand. wowinside

writer and dramatist. Things didn't go quite as the couple might have expected. Sand had picked up typhoid in Genoa and was forced to stay in bed at the Hotel Danieli, while de Musset checked into the Hotel Europa. They argued, he entertained himself with various prostitutes and then ended up in bed with typhoid. A doctor was called, Sand fell in love with him, de Musset returned to Paris and Sand and the doctor had a passionate affair.

Sand loved Venice and the freedom it gave her. She wrote in her autobiography that in contrast with other cities that felt like prisons, she loved Venice for what it was, the calm that it transmitted on clear days, and the dark shadows of its storms.[46]

Charles Dickens in Venice

Charles Dickens first came to Venice in November 1844 and stayed at the Hotel Daniele. He'd gone to Italy in July earlier in the year, tired from writing novels and in need of a break. He went to Genoa with his wife Catherine and their five children, and while he was there he decided to spend some time seeing Italy. When he arrived in Venice that night it seemed to him a dream-like, ghostly city, almost funereal. When he woke the next morning, he was treated to clear skies and the shining beauty of Venice. 'Nothing in the world that you have ever heard of Venice is equal to the magnificent and stupendous reality,' he wrote in his *Pictures from Italy* (1846). 'Venice is beyond the fancy of the wildest dreamer.'[47]

Petrarch and Venice

In 1362 Francesco Petrarca, or Petrarch as we know him in English, arrived in Venice. He'd been living in Milan when the plague broke out and so in 1361, he left Milan and fled to Padua. He then went on to Venice, where he lived in the Palazzo Molin Delle Due Torri (Palazzo Molin of the Two Towers) with his daughter Francesca and her family. He was given use of the house by the Venetian senate under the condition that after his death he would leave his library to the Republic. Petrarch lived there with his daughter, son-in-law and grandchild[48] for about five years between 1362 and 1367. Petrarch was incredibly important as a writer, not just for Italian literature

Charles Dickens. nickolae

Petrarch. Georgios Kollidas

but for European literature. He was a poet and an influence on Shakespeare, but most importantly he was the father of Renaissance Humanism, a new way of thinking that placed the individual rather than the church at its centre. Look out for the plaque on the building's façade near the San Sepulcro bridge. Giovanni Boccaccio, whose most famous work was *The Decameron* (1353), visited Petrarch at his home in Venice twice and stayed for several months. Petrarch, Dante and Boccaccio are considered some of the most important writers in Italian literature.

Riva degli Schiavoni, 4145

Chiesa Della Pietà and Vivaldi

If you had walked past here in the first part of the eighteenth century, you would have quite possibly heard music coming from the Pio Ospedale della Pietà, the orphanage for girls that was once here. Babies were posted through the wall by mothers who were unable to keep them. The nuns took them in and raised them. The most talented musicians became part of the *figlie di coro*, the girls who were specially selected for the orchestra there. Newly ordained priest Antonio Vivaldi worked here as violin teacher and then director of the music school from 1703 to 1740,

Santa Maria della Pietà church. Dietmar

and while he was here, he wrote his most famous work *The Four Seasons* (1723). If you want to learn more about the life of the girls who lived here, then read Harriet Constable's *The Instrumentalist* (2024). It's inspired by the story of one of his students, the violinist Anna Maria della Pietà, and asks the question: how much did the girls contribute to or were influential in Vivaldi's music? Barbara Quick takes the same story of Anna Maria and gives it a slightly different twist in her novel *Vivaldi's Virgins* (2007). In her novel, Anna Maria Dal Violin sets out to look for her parents. The orphanage has now gone and what we see now is the Chiesa di Santa Maria della Pietà church, but the interest in the history of the girls of the Pio Ospedale della Pietà remains.

Castello, 3701 Riva degli Schiavoni

Chiesa Di San Franceso Della Vigna and Veronica Franco

'Oh, God, save us from whore poetesses! They are more boring than their clients,' says the courtesan Fiammetta in the novel *In the Company of the Courtesan* (2006)[49] to her faithful man servant Bucino. Unless you happen to be Veronica Franco, of course, one of

San Francesco della Vigna church. Renáta Sedmáková

the most fascinating and distinguished courtesans in Venice.

The Chiesa di San Francesco della Vigna in the Campo di San Francesco della Vigna is where the sixteenth-century courtesan Franco was buried when she died in 1591 at the age of 45. She was born in 1546. Her mother had been a courtesan before getting married and starting a family, and when Veronica was born, she decided that she would teach her how to optimise her charms and beauty to make a good marriage. At the same time, Veronica joined her brothers' lessons and was able to get herself an education, which was unusual for girls at the time. When her father died, Franco married a wealthy doctor while she was still a teen, but he was violent, and she asked for a separation. It was then that she decided to become a courtesan, alongside her mother who had returned to the trade. Franco was beautiful, intelligent, cultured and an accomplished musician, and became a courtesan to rich and powerful patricians. We can imagine her sitting in her palazzo dressed in her dress made from the finest fabrics, a low neckline with possibly her breasts exposed, and a string of pearls around her neck. There was a period where pearls, the symbol of innocence, were forbidden, but courtesans wore them anyway. When she went out, she would have worn the Venetian high wooden platform shoes, the *calcagnette*. The higher the shoe, the higher the status, and Franco was at the very top of her profession. In a similar way, her skirts would have been very full as if to create her own stage, as Sarah Dunant tells us in *In the Company of the Courtesan* (2006) when she describes the courtesans walking into church.

Franco was a *cortegiana onesta*, an 'honest courtesan', the highest level, and engaged with Venetian society on both a social, intellectual and political level. She featured at the top of the city's catalogue of courtesans of 1565, where she was noted for her ability to write poetry.[50] She commanded high fees and was highly skilled at writing sensual poetry, which she used to seduce her clients. When Henry Valois, who later became Henry III of France, spent a night in Venice in summer 1574, it was with Franco, and we know that he took an enamel portrait of her and two of her poems with him back to France.

Franco wrote two volumes of poetry from a distinctly protofeminist perspective on topics such as philosophy and politics, and daily life.[51] She lived in a palazzo in the parish of Santa Maria Formosa, where she also held her salon. Nobles, writer and artists gathered to discuss the cultural issues of the day. Later, Franco was accused of witchcraft and heresy. This was the sixteenth century and all over Europe women were being accused of being witches by neighbours, enemies and those who had taken a dislike to them for whatever reason. While so-called witches were never burned at the stake in Venice, they still faced public humiliation, heavy penalties, and a miserable future. Franco defended herself with great skill and awareness of language, and the charges were eventually dropped, possibly because Domenico Venier and his nephew Marco, with whom Franco had also had a relationship, were able to help and advise her. Domenico was from one of the oldest Venetian patrician families and a Venetian poet. He lived at Ca' Venier, Palazzo Venier dei Leoni, where the Guggenheim collection is housed. He held his famous literary salon there, which Franco attended, and Venier became her patron and encouraged her to write poetry.

After the publication of Franco's second volume of poetry in 1580, we have very little information about her, which suggests that her economic situation may have deteriorated. We know that she set up a home for ex-prostitutes and other 'fallen women' as they were known at the time, the Ospizio del Soccorso along the Fondamenta del Soccorso in Dorsoduro, and it's possible that she too decided to change her life.

Castello, 2786, Calle S. Francesco

Elena Cassandra Tarabotti

When Elena Cassandra Tarabotti was born in Castello in 1604 and it turned out she had a limp, her father gave up hopes of finding a good marriage for her and destined her for the convent.

The convent was the Benedictine convent of Sant'Anna, which was where the Sant'Anna church is along the Fondamenta Sant'Anna. It's thought that she could have been as young as 11 when she entered the convent. She was given the name of Archangela and spent the rest of her life there, where she started to write. Elena too was a protofeminist who felt the situation of women deeply. Her work *Inferno Monacale* (1643), literally Convent Hell, which she published herself, told the truth about women's lives in the convents, where girls were closed away against their will, just as Elena was closed away herself.

Libreria Acqua Alta

Libreria Acqua Alta is one of the most photographed and well-known bookshops in the world. We've all seen the pictures of this small bookshop along the canal, with books piled high everywhere and on every available surface. It was opened in 2002 by Luigi Frizzo. You'll find it along Calle Santa Maria Formosa, not far from the church of the same name.

Libreria Acqua Alta, Calle Santa Maria Formosa, 5176b, www.libreriaacquaalta.it

The Cemetery Island of San Michele and Ezra Pound

The cemetery island of San Michele is where American poet Ezra Pound was buried in the non-Catholic

Island of San Michele. Aerial Film Studio

section when he died in 1972. Pound is an extremely controversial figure because of his fascist and anti-Semitic beliefs. He lived in Venice for twelve years with violinist Olga Rudge before his death. A single gondola with four gondoliers took him to his final resting place, and no tribute was made by either the Italian or US government.[52]

Pound had first come to Venice in 1908 and lived near Ponte San Vio, where he took a room. He was 22, fresh from a broken engagement, had tried an academic career, and arrived in Venice with dreams of literary success. He took lodgings in Dorsoduro near Fondamenta Nani, where he published his first volume of poems *A Lume Spento* (1908). Later he lived nearby at Calle Querini, 252.

Olga had bought the apartment in 1928. She and Pound had met at American heiress Natalie Barney's salon in Paris in autumn 1922. Olga was a young and very gifted violinist, and they started an affair that would last until Pound's death in 1972. Pound was married to artist Dorothy Shakespear and had been since 1914, and in fact she would outlive him by a year. During the Second World War, Pound, Dorothy and Olga all lived together, while Pound broadcast support for Hitler and Mussolini to the US. In 1945 he was arrested and charged with treason against his country. The verdict was that he was insane, and he spent twelve years in a psychiatric hospital in Washington DC. He returned to Italy in 1958 and spent much of the rest of his life there with Olga.

The Darker Side of Venice

The darker side of Venice has appealed to many writers and made for some great thrillers along the way. Venice is a labyrinth of streets where it's easy to get lost, and while you might find it perfectly charming on a warm summer's evening, it can take on a totally different aspect when the days get shorter, and the fog comes in. Daphne du Maurier's story *Don't Look Now* (1971) is a classic and was made into a film two years later. Patricia Highsmith set her novel *Those Who Walk Away* (1967) here, and Philip Gwynne Jones wrote his series about Honorary English Consul Nathan Sunderland, who works along the Street of the Assassins and is drawn into Venetian mysteries. Muriel Spark's *Territorial Rights* (1979) is about two men following each other around Venice, going down dead ends and not being able to escape, while Michael Dibdin's *Dead Lagoon* (1994) plays beautifully on the idea of the dead lagoon or Laguna Morta to the north of the Venetian lagoon.

synthetick

natasenko

5

SOUTH OF THE GRAND CANAL

DORSODURO

Dorsoduro literally means 'hard back' as there were fewer marshes here and the land was harder and more compact. It's to the south of the Grand Canal along with the districts of San Polo and Santa Croce, and includes the island of Giudecca that faces it to the south. Giudecca is where the Venetian nobles had their villas with gardens and vineyards and where they used to go for parties and other social events. This is also the location of the

Dorsoduro. Anna Reinert

Fondamenta delle Zattere, Dorsoduro. Elena Dijour

famous luxury Hotel Cipriani, which was opened in 1956 by Giuseppe Cipriani. Jan Morris describes it as it was during the 1970s in her essay *Let Her Sink* (1975), published in the *New York Times*. She writes of walking back through Dorsoduro with its old palaces and pigeons and the type of Venetian boat known as a *sandalo*, like a gondola but with a flat bottom.

Dorsoduro is where you'll find some of the city's universities, so it's more student focused. It's home to some of Venice's most important art galleries, including the Peggy Guggenheim Collection and the Galleria dell'Accademia. It's also a great place to come for an aperitivo or a meal. Head to one of the bars and restaurants all along the Fondamenta delle Zattere or to Campo Santa Margherita in the centre of the *sestiere*. Take your book and read on about the writers who stayed here and loved it all so much.

Gondolas

Percy Shelley called them the most 'beautiful and convenient boats in the world' in a letter to wife Mary on

muratart

23 August 1818. He delighted in their soft black furnishings, black because of a series of laws that had been imposed. At the time each gondola had a small cabin, and Shelley loved the decorated glass and black blinds that could be pulled down.[1] The blinds also hid a multitude of sins. In Sarah Dunant's *In the Company of the Courtesan* (2006), the courtesan Fiammetta and her man servant toy with the idea of a gondola for Fiammetta to work from as a cheaper alternative to renting a house. Byron loved the gondolas and wrote that all Venice's 'disadvantages are more than compensated by the sight of a gondola'. When writer Thomas Coryat arrived at the beginning of the seventeenth century, gondolas were still covered by a wooden vault with benches covered in black leather and decorated with linen and lace.[2] When Oscar Wilde went to Venice with his tutor from Trinity College Dublin, John Pentland Mahaffy, the gondolas reminded him of funeral barges, like that in which the dead King Arthur was taken away. Henry James described that of the Hotel Europa as a hearse.[3] He was upset when his gondolier decided to sing badly and

feared that the old Venice was lost. Luckily, the view of the Grand Canal reassured him that it wasn't.

Dorsoduro is home to one of the last gondola boatyards, Lo Squero di San Trovaso, which has been here since the seventeenth century. For visits and guided tours see *www.squerosantrovaso.com*

Jan Morris's Venice

At the end of the 1950s Jan Morris, who was writing and living under the name of James Morris but identified as a woman, came to Venice to write a book. It wasn't the first time Morris had been to Venice. The first and previous time was in 1945 as an 18-year-old intelligence officer in the British Army, when his assigned duties were helping with running the motorboats in Venice. With Venice, it was a case of love at first sight. When Morris came back with his wife and children in the 1950s, they all stayed in a flat near the Accademia Gallery in the courtyard and employed a local woman named Emilia to help with cooking and housework. Life settled into a quiet provincial routine; the family went

rh2010

out and explored Venice in their small boat, while a trip to Harry's Bar was an occasional treat. The resulting book was *Venice* (1960), which explores, the city's culture, history and so much more and was an international bestseller. Morris was also well-known for her transition from male to female, which took place in 1972, and she wrote her book *Conundrum* (1974) about it.

Literary Palazzos

Palazzo Giustinian Brandolin and a Golden Summer

Gill Johnson's memoir *Love from Venice: A Golden Summer on the Grand Canal* (2024) takes us back to the days of the Venice season, when aristocrats, film stars, writers and others of the international jet set descended every summer on Venice, specifically during late August and early September around the time of the Venice Film Festival. It's a fascinating insight into the world of Venice during the 1950s before the days of mass tourism.

In the summer of 1957, Johnson went to Venice to take up a job in the home of Count Brandino Brandolini d'Adda and the Countess Cristiana from the Agnelli family of the Fiat car manufacturing empire in Turin. She spent her time teaching English to their two sons and stayed in the family's fifteenth-century Gothic Palazzo Brandolin near

the Accademia Bridge along the Grand Canal, also known as Palazzo Giustinian. She was also invited for tea on Aristotle Onassis's luxury yacht, Christina O. In the summer she took the boys to the Lido and the private beach of the Hotel Excelsior, where a four-course lunch arrived for herself and the boys with butlers in white gloves, who set up a table on the beach. When the season ended, the people from the Brandolinis' circle left the city and returned to their homes on the mainland, and Johnson and the family went to their country home near Udine. One of the highlights of Johnson's stay was when she was invited to spend the night at Palazzo Papadopoli with the Count's sister, Grazia Gonzaga. Palazzo Papadopoli used to belong to the Tiepolo family, and she was invited into Gonzaga's bedroom to see some paintings. As she looked at the four walls painted with cherubs and clouds, flowers and saints, she realised they were by Tiepolo, the famous Venetian artist. As Johnson points out, most people travel to museums to see Tiepolo, whereas Grazia saw them every morning when she woke up. Johnson wrote the book on the encouragement of her son after she found the letters she had written to her husband from Venice after his death. He had kept them all.

Dorsoduro 3228 Calle Giustinian

Palazzo Papadopoli. BasPhoto

Palazzo Venier Dei Leoni

Palazzo Venier dei Leoni was once home to the Veniers, one of the most powerful and richest families in Venice. Going by the original plans by architect Lorenzo Boschetti in 1749 it was supposed to have five floors. We don't know exactly why, but only one was built. It's this that nowadays makes it distinctive; this low, one-floor palazzo that is now home to the Peggy Guggenheim Collection, one of the first modern art collections. It's also known for three women who lived here, Luisa Casati, Lady Doris Castlerosse, and Peggy Guggenheim, who you can read about in the following section. Judith Mackrell brings all three of these women together in her book *The Unfinished Palazzo* (2017), a must-read if you're planning to visit.

Casati, the Marchesa Casati, was the first of the three women to take residence in Palazzo Venier. She rented it in 1910 for three years and gave legendary parties where guests arrived in gondolas dressed in oriental costumes. There were parrots and monkeys in cages in the salon, and a semi-wild cheetah roamed the garden with white peacocks and pedigree greyhounds.[4] Casati inspired Jack Kerouac, Marcel Proust, Ezra Pound and Tennessee Williams among others, and had a relationship with Italian poet and playwright Gabriele d'Annunzio. His home, the Casetta Rossa, was opposite Casati's palazzo on the other side of the Grand Canal. D'Annunzio was certainly a character to match Casati, and known for his collection of erotic poetry, *Intermezzo di Rime* (1883).

Lady Doris Castlerosse, born Doris Delevingne, moved to Palazzo Venier in 1938. She had had affairs with some of the richest and most powerful men in London, had married Viscount Castlerosse in 1928, got bored of him, and escaped to Venice in summer 1932. In Venice, she joined a rich and entertaining set that included Cecil Beaton and Noel Coward. Castlerosse was also friends with American heiress Margot Liddon Flick Hoffman. When she had the idea of taking over Palazzo Venier, Margot gave her the financial backing. The palazzo needed extensive refurbishment before it could be lived in, as the previous owner had started the work but then ran out of money. In 1936, building work began, and in summer 1938 Castlerosse opened Palazzo Venier. Castelerosse wanted to make a name for herself as a Venetian hostess, and she gave parties all that summer with her society and literary friends. It was the only summer she would spend there. In 1939 war broke out and Castlerosse never returned to Venice. American composer and songwriter Cole Porter immortalised Castlerosse and the Venetian way of life during the war in his song *Where is the Life that Late I Led?* in his stage musical *Kiss me Kate* (1948). Venetia in the song is a reference to Castlerosse, who he sings about as still drinking in her palazzo.

Peggy Guggenheim Collection, Dorsoduro, 701

Peggy Guggenheim

Twentieth-century art collector Peggy Guggenheim once said that 'To live in Venice or even to visit it means that you fall in love with the city itself. There is nothing left over in your heart for anyone else.' Guggenheim bought the Palazzo Venier dei Leoni in 1948. She'd visited Venice several times, fallen in love with the city and was now fulfilling her dream of living in Venice and finding a home for her art collection. It was the same year that Venice's international art exhibition, the Venice Biennale, was relaunched. Her timing couldn't have been better. She was offered the Greek pavilion and rented an apartment at the top of Palazzo Barbaro where Henry James had written *The Aspern Papers* (1888). In 1951 she opened her museum at Palazzo Venier. Writers such as Gore Vidal and Tennessee Williams came to visit, and Truman Capote stayed with her in 1949 while he worked on his memoir *The Muses are Heard* (1956). Guggenheim became known for being photographed in her gondola with her trademark butterfly-frame glasses and was known as the *Dogaressa* or wife of the Doge as a mark of respect.

Jane Turner Rylands

Although Jane Turner Rylands has never lived at the Palazzo Venier, her husband was the director of the Peggy Guggenheim Collection in Venice for thirty-five years. Rylands came to Venice in 1973 and has lived here ever since. She's written two collections of short stories about the city, *Venetian Stories* (2003), twelve stories about the lives of Venetians, and *Across the Bridge of Sighs: More Venetian Stories* (2007).

Palazzo Loredan Dell'ambasciatore and Giustiniana Wynne

Palazzo Loredan is where writer Giustiniana Wynne lived with her husband Count Rosenberg, the elderly Austrian ambassador, before they went to Austria.

Wynne was an Anglo-Venetian writer who lived from 1737 to 1791. She got pregnant when she was unmarried while living in Paris in 1755. How it was all dealt with was revealed in Giacomo Casanova's memoirs, published after both his and Wynne's deaths in 1822. Casanova had initially tried to procure her the means to provoke an abortion, but this was unsuccessful, and he eventually found her a place in a convent, where she had the baby. There is no trace of the baby

Palazzo Loredan. wjarek

and Giustiniana never once mentioned the episode in any of her letters.

When Giustiniana married Count Rosenberg in 1761, he was 70 and she was 24. By this time, she wasn't expecting to marry, and the offer came as a surprise. She accepted, and when he died she received an income for life upon which she could live reasonably. In this she was a woman of her time and understood perfectly both her options and her limitations.[5] After the count's death she returned to Italy. It was then that she started to write. She wrote three books, including an account of a Venetian celebration and a novel, *Les Morlacques* (1788), which she wrote in French, about the Morlach people of Dalmatia.

Giustiniana was the illegitimate daughter of a Venetian mother, who then married a Protestant English baronet who legalised her birth. Her story is explored in Andrea di Robilant's book *A Venetian Affair: A True Tale of Forbidden Love in the 18th Century* (2003). In the introduction to his book, Di Robilant writes how some years before him writing the book his father found some letters in a box in the attic of Palazzo Mocenigo. His great grandmother was Valentina Mocenigo, hence the link. They were love letters written by Andrea Memmo to Giustiniana. Memmo belonged to one of the old aristocratic Venetian families of the Golden Book, the book that provided an official record of patrician lineage, and a love affair with anyone outside the patrician families was totally forbidden. If their relationship had been discovered, he would have lost any chance of a political career, his children would have been denied patrician status, and he could have been disinherited by his family. Giustiniana's letters had been found during the 1920s in Padua, and more were found at the Randolph Macon College in the US. The missing link had always been Andrea's letters, and here they were to finally give the other side of the story.

Dorsoduro 1262/A Calle Dei Cerchieri

Lucia: A Venetian Life in the Age of Napoleon

Lucia: A Venetian Life in the Age of Napoleon (2009) is also by Andrea di Robilant. It tells the story of Lucia, a Venetian noblewoman who was also Byron's landlady. Her father was Andrea Memmo, who had been the lover of Giustiniana Wynne. Memmo married his daughter off to Alvise Mocenigo, after he'd consulted the Golden Book to find an appropriate match. At the time the family were living in Naples, where Andrea was the Venetian Ambassador and struggling financially, and then Lucia went back to Venice as Alvise's wife. Her life then unfolds to the historical backdrop of the end of the Republic, its fall to Napoleon and the ensuing occupation. The book is based on the series of letters that Lucia wrote to her fiancé Andrea while they were engaged, and a larger body of letters, those that Lucia wrote to her sister Paulina, through five decades of their lives.

Ca' Rezzonico

Robert Browning always wanted to buy his own palazzo in Venice but never did. He looked at buying the Palazzo Contarini da Zaffo, which was near the Accademia, but was unsuccessful. His son Pen, as he was always known, married the wealthy American heiress Fannie Coddington in October 1887. In 1888 Pen bought his own Venetian palazzo, the seventeenth-century Ca' Rezzonico along the Grand Canal, which today is a museum dedicated to eighteenth-century Venice. Robert Browning came to stay here, and spent time between here, London and staying with Katherine de Kay Bronson at her home on the mainland in Asolo. When he came to Ca' Rezzonico in autumn 1889, he caught a cold that turned into something far more severe and on 12 December 1889 he died. For years the idea had been that after his death Browning would be taken to Florence and buried with his

Ca' Rezzonico. Marco Taliani

wife, Elizabeth Barret Browning, but that didn't happen as the cemetery had shut down. Instead, Browning was taken to London and buried in Westminster Abbey in Poets' Corner near Tennyson. Outside on the wall of Ca' Rezzonico there is a plaque that commemorates Browning. It has the quote from his poem *De Gustibus* (1855): 'Open my heart and you will see/Graved inside it "Italy".' Songwriter Cole Porter rented the palazzo between 1926 and 1927, and held wild and scandalous parties with cocktails, cocaine, rent boys and gondoliers to serve the drinks.

Dorsoduro, 3136 Fondamenta Rezzonico

Palazzo Orio Semitecolo Benzon and Constance Fenimore Woolson

When successful novelist Constance Fenimore Woolson fell from the windows of Palazzo Semitecolo on 24 January 1894, the question was whether she jumped or fell. It's a question we still don't really know the answer to, although her friend Henry James believed it was suicide. She was 53 when she died.

Woolson was a writer of novels, shorts stories and poems, and grandniece of the writer James Fenimore Cooper. *For the Major* (1883) was possibly her most famous work, about the south of the United States in the years just after the Civil War. She had left the United States after her mother died in 1879 and moved to Europe, where she lived in various places. At the time of her death, she was living in Venice. What we do know about the time before her death is that she was depressed, and that she and Henry James had become close. Had she fallen in love with him? In which case, it could have been a case of unrequited love as there are suggestions that James may have been gay. In any case, James was keen to go through her personal possessions after her death and ensure that his letters to her were burned.[6] It also signified the end of James' love for Venice. He only came back to Venice twice after that, once in 1899 and the last time in 1907.

Dorsoduro, 187 Calle del Bastion

Chiesa Di San Pantalon and Lucrezia Marinelli

You'll find the church of San Pantalon in the Campo di San Pantalon near Campo Santa Margherita where all

San Pantalon church. Gabriele Maltinti

the bars and cafés are. It's where writer and poet Lucrezia Marinelli was buried. Marinelli was born in 1571. Her father was a physician and philosopher, and she had a good home environment in which to study and learn. We know that she married a physician and had two children, and that she was able to dedicate herself to her studies and her writing. She lived a reclusive life, although at the time most women did. Life was generally very limited for Venetian women, and so writing was often a way of engaging with the world on their terms. She is best known for her book *The Nobility and Excellence of Women and the Defects and Vices of Men* (1600). It was a response to a Giuseppe Passi's *I Donneschi Difetti* (The Defects of Women), which had been published in Venice a year earlier. Marinelli listed the defects and put forward her defence. During this period there was a lively debate going on about women, a dialogue that went backwards and forwards between men and women who were writers at the time and resulted in some of the first protofeminist texts. Moderata Fonte's *The Worth of Women: Wherein is Clearly Revealed Their Nobility and Their Superiority to Men* (1600) was published posthumously by Fonte's daughter in the same year.

Dorsoduro, 3703

Gaspara Stampa

Gaspara Stampa was considered one of the most important woman poets during the middle of the sixteenth century. She lived with her sister Cassandra in the parish of Saints Gervasio and Protasio, now known as San Trovaso, in the district of Dorsoduro. She was born in Padua in 1523, but her father died when she was a girl and so the family went to live in their mother's hometown of Venice. Gaspara and Cassandra were both excellent musicians. They sang and played the lute, which was the

Gaspara Stampa. Wikimedia Commons

Fondamenta delle Zattere. Peter

popular instrument of the time. Their home became a cultural meeting place for writers and musicians, yet it was for her words that Gaspara would be remembered. Some of her most famous poetry dates to the period after her brother's death in 1554. Gaspara wanted to become a nun but fell in love with Count Collaltino di Collalto. Their relationship lasted for three years, and it inspired some of her most beautiful poems; more than three hundred of them, which she dedicated to him. The couple never married, and Stampa died when she was only 31 in 1554. You can find her poems in English online, so should you feel it's time for a cappuccino in one of the cafés along the waterfront, this is the perfect moment to read some of her work and allow yourself to be transported back in time.

Pensione Accademia

The Pensione Accademia is where American poet and journalist Cynthia Zaran is writing from when she opens her book *In Italy* (2023), the first chapter of which is about Venice. She tells us how she doesn't often visit new places, and goes to Venice to 'retrace my steps, looking for breadcrumbs I left long ago that were since eaten by the birds'.[7] She starts to remember how she came to Venice at 19 with a boy and sat on the steps of the Santa Maria della Salute Basilica on the Punta della Dogana. They ate pressed veal sandwiches and drank *aranciata* or orange soda from cans. She thought she might get married to the boy but didn't. At the time they didn't stay in Venice because it was too expensive and stayed in Padua instead.

Exiled Russian poet and essayist Joseph Brodsky also used to stay here when he came to Venice. He visited many times in the winter, spent the first Christmas that he was in exile here and the last before his death in January 1996. His essay *Watermark: An Essay on Venice* (1989) really captures that winter atmosphere. Zarin and Brodsky knew each other. When she comes to Venice, she writes how she goes to look for her friend's grave and eventually finds it in the Protestant cemetery on San Michele Island. Brodsky died in New York but was buried in Venice at the request of his wife, Maria Sozzani.

Dorsoduro, 1058 Fondamenta Bollani, www.pensioneaccademia.it

Basilica Santa Maria della Salute. zm_photo

Fondamenta Delle Zattere

Fondamenta delle Zattere is the long walkway that stretches along the waterfront of Dorsoduro. 'Fondamenta' is the street that runs parallel to a canal. 'Zattere' means rafts, and it refers to the rafts that carpenters used to transport logs. The walkway stretches from San Basilio as far as Punta della Dogana where the old customs house was, now home to the Pinault Collection, which hosts temporary art exhibitions. Henry James used to stay here at Casa Biondetti near the Basilica di Santa Maria di Salute, known to the locals as the Salute. Historian Rawdon Brown, a friend of the Ruskins, also lived along here at number 560. It's where Julia Garnet in Sally Vickers' novel *Miss Garnet's Angel* (2000) rents her apartment that she found via an agency from the holiday section in *The Guardian* after the death of her friend Harriet and begins to question her life.

John Addington Symonds

Victorian poet John Addington Symonds rented Ca' Torresella along the Fondamenta delle Zattere. He was married and had four children. He had an affair with a gondolier, as did poet A.E. Housman. Back home in England, the death penalty for sexual relations between men had only been abolished in 1861, yet the sentence was still a minimum of ten years' imprisonment. In contrast, Venice was more tolerant, and Symonds spent a lot of time in

Fondamenta delle Zattere. fottoo

Venice during his life. His presumed lover was Angelo Fanto, who he met on the Lido, a known place for meeting gay lovers. Horatio Brown had an affair with a gondolier named Antonio Salin, and he dedicated his book *Life on the Lagoons* (1884) to him. Lord Ronald Gower, on the other hand, was very open about being gay when he came to Venice and joined their social circle. He provided the inspiration for Lord Henry Wootton in *The Picture of Dorian Gray* by Oscar Wilde.[8]

Accademia Di Belle Arti and Sylvia Pankhurst

The Accademia di Belle Arti is the academy of fine arts in Venice, and is where English writer, artist and suffragette Sylvia Pankhurst came to study art in Venice. She was the second daughter of Emmeline Pankhurst and had been granted a travel scholarship to study art by Owen's College in Manchester, which would later become Manchester University. She came out to Venice in 1902 and stayed at the palazzo of Polish countess Sophie Bertelli Algarotti in Calle de l'Arco in the parish of Sant'Antonio in Castello. She loved her art and took part in the literary and artistic *salons* at Sophie's house, but then in 1903 her family asked her to go back to Manchester.[9] Sylvia embraced the suffragette movement. She was an editor and a writer of pamphlets, including *Save the*

Accademia di Belle Arti. AlexMastro

ACCADEMIA
DI BELLE ARTI
Gallerie
Accademia,
Venezia
GALLERIE

Mothers (1930), her plea for a national health service that would provide good-quality antenatal and obstetrics care for women at a time when 3,000 women and 20,000 babies were dying each year in England and Wales. She also wrote a collection of poems, *Writ on Cold Slate* (1922), about her experiences in Holloway prison. Nearby Pensione Seguso is where Patricia Highsmith once stayed on the advice of an artist who she met in Positano, and it features in her novel *Those Who Walk Away* (1967).

Dorsoduro, 423, Fondamenta Zattere allo Spirito Santo, www.accademiavenezia.it

Muriel Spark

Scottish writer Muriel Spark first came to Venice in February 1975 and stayed in lodgings near the Accademia di Belle Arti. She too favoured Venice in winter and autumn. It's also the season in which she sets her novel *Territorial Rights* (1979) in Venice. In the late 1970s Venice of her novel, it's a quieter time where it's much easier to keep on meeting people in the street, and this is what happens in the novel. Spark eventually settled in Italy, moving to Rome for many years and then to Orvieto in Tuscany during the 1980s, where she died in 2006. For Spark, the question was not what you think of Venice, but how it makes you feel.

La Calcina Bridge. marcelinopozo

Café La Calcina

Caffè La Calcina, or Hotel La Calcina as it's called now, is along the part of the Fondamenta Zattere known as Fondamenta delle Zattere ai Gesuiti, to the left of the Ponte della Calcina as you're standing in front of the bridge. John Ruskin stayed in the rooms here in spring 1877 when he was suffering from periods of madness because of a brain dysfunction known as encephalopathy. His rooms were at the front and overlooked the Giudecca Canal.

Dorsoduro, 780 www.lacalcina.com

SAN POLO

San Polo takes its name from Campo San Polo, Venice's largest square after that of San Marco, and the church of the same name. This is where you'll find the Rialto Bridge, and the area around it known as the Rialto, that stretches across the districts of San Marco and San Polo. It's named after the *sestiere* San Marco's original name of Rivoalto, which then became Rialto. Look out for the statue to Carlo Goldoni in Campo Bartolomeo. He's Venice's most famous playwright and knew Casanova's mother as she acted in his plays. Also take a walk down La Frezzeria, which is where Byron lived just after he arrived in Venice. He originally stayed at the Hotel Great Britain on the Grand Canal but then moved into apartments above a draper's shop, where he quickly had a passionate affair with the landlord's wife.

The Rialto Bridge

The Grand Canal is crossed by four bridges, one of which is the Rialto that connects the districts of San Marco and San Polo.

Campo San Polo. Aliaksandr Campo

It's specifically mentioned in Shakespeare's *The Merchant of Venice* (1600). Act Three scene One begins with Salanio, Antonio's close friend, asking another friend Salarino: What news on the Rialto? Salarino is referring to the district of Rialto; the bridge itself wasn't built until the end of the sixteenth century. At the time the Rialto was known as the financial and commercial centre of Venice, and as Venice's red-light district. During the fifteenth century the Venetian Republic had opened brothels to keep the prostitutes out of the centre here in the area near the Ponte delle Tette and the Fondamenta delle Tette in the parish of San Cassiano. Ponte delle Tette literally means the Bridge of the Tits and is where women used to stand on the bridge or sit on the windowsills of the brothels with their breasts on display, and often their legs positioned to show what was

San Polo and the San Stin Bridge. travelview

The Rialto Bridge. hungry_herbivore

under their skirts. Tom Ripley stays at a hotel near the Rialto Bridge when he goes to Venice.

Take a walk around the food markets, which are some of the oldest in Venice, and are still popular today with restaurants and local people. Elizabeth David wrote about the fish market back in her book *Italian Food* (1954), where 'sardines shine like newly minted coins, pink Venetian scampi are fat and fresh, infinitely enticing in the early dawn'.[10] Cantina do Mori is near the Rialto and is a typical *bacaro* or small tavern. It's been open since 1462 and is where Casanova used to take his lovers. Try their house specialty, the *francobolli* sandwiches.

Cantina do Mori, San Polo, 429 Calle do Mori

The Rialto fish market. Ilia Baksheev

Carlo Goldoni, Venice's Most Famous Playwright

Carlo Goldoni was born on 25 February in 1707 in Ca' Centanni in Campo San Cassino. He studied for a law degree at the University of Padua, started writing plays and became involved with the Sant'Angelo Theatre, one of the most important theatres in Venice at the time. He's remembered not just for his plays but for how he made changes within the theatre. At the time actors always wore masks, whereas Goldoni got rid of these and revealed their faces. In 1750, he wrote sixteen plays in total for the new theatre season, some of which are still performed all over the world. When he moved to the San Luca theatre in 1753, he created more change when he started to write about the middle classes. Whereas previously plays had focused on patricians, Goldoni now portrayed everyday people's lives. The house is now a museum, which you can visit to learn about his life.

San Polo, 2794 Rio Terà dei Nomboli, www.carlogoldoni.visitmuve.it

Statue of Carlo Goldoni in Campo San Bartolomeo.
andersphoto

Literary Palazzos

Palazzo Albrizzi and Isabella Teotochi Albrizzi

Isabella Teotochi Albrizzi's cultural and literary *ridotto* or salon was known throughout Europe and beyond.

She was born in Corfu into a family of nobles, and at the age of 16 she married the Venetian Carlo Antonio Marin and moved to Venice, where she developed a love of literature and culture and started to host her own literary salon. When Byron arrived in Venice in 1816, Albrizzi was in her fifties and a widow. Byron soon entered Venetian life and became a regular at her salon. Albrizzi was an author in her own right. She wrote *Ritratti* (1807) with Gasparo Gozzi, and a description of 148 works by Antonio Canova (1809). Canova liked her book so much her gave her a sculpture. French writer Madame de Staël held Europe's most

Madame de Staël. Georgios Kollidas

important salon in Paris, and when she first came to Venice, she came to Albrizzi's salon.

San Polo, 1939 Campiello Albrizzi

Bianca Cappello and Thomas Middleton

Not far from the Rialto market is the Palazzo Cappello along Calle Bianca Cappello già del Ponte Storto, where Venetian noblewoman Bianca Capello was born in 1548. Bianca's parents were Bartolomeo Capello and Pellegrina Morosini, who came from two of Venice's oldest and most important families. Pellegrina died when Bianca was 10 and Bianca's father remarried but Bianca had a difficult relationship with her stepmother. Later Bianca claimed that her stepmother was one of the reasons why when she was only 15, she met a young Florentine clerk named Pietro Bonaventura and ran away to Florence with him. It all created a huge scandal, and a reward was offered for killing Bonaventura and bringing Bianca home. A diplomatic crisis between Venice and Tuscany was just about avoided, the Grand Duke of Tuscany Cosimo I offered the couple protection, and they settled down to a far more modest life than Bianca had been used to.

Several years passed, and Francesco I de' Medici became Grand Duke of Tuscany. He was married of course, nevertheless he fell in love with Bianca and installed her as his official mistress. Then after his wife's early death, he married Bianca at the Palazzo Vecchio in Florence. The Venetian authorities, the same authorities that had tried to have Bianca arrested after she ran off to Florence with the clerk, now changed their tune. They all attended the wedding as they couldn't possibly upset the Grand Duke of Tuscany, and Bianca became the Grand Duchess. Moderata Fonte wrote the poems for their wedding, *I Tredici Canti del Floridoro* (1581). Bianca's story inspired English playwright Thomas Middleton's tragedy *Women Beware Women* (1657). Bianca becomes Livia, is already married to a Florentine clerk, is seduced by the duke and becomes his mistress. Of course, the story is a tragedy with no happy ending, so everyone dies at the end and Livia kills herself by drinking from a poisoned chalice.

San Polo, Calle Bianca Capello

Palazzo Dandolo

The Calle del Ridotto is where the old Palazzo Dandolo was near the church of San Moisè. Marco Dandolo opened the first public gaming house known as a *ridotto* in this palazzo in 1638. Francesco Guardi's painting *The Ridotto Pubblico at Palazzo Dandolo*, brings to life the *ridotto* in the middle of the eighteenth century when Casanova was a regular and enormous sums of money were at stake.

San Polo, 2879

Dante Alighieri at the Palazzo Soranzo

Italian poet Dante Alighieri went to Venice as a guest of Doge Giovanni Soranzo in 1321. He was there as ambassador for Guido Novello da Polenta. Da Polenta had invited Dante to stay with him in Ravenna when he was banished from Florence after the Black Guelphs won the war in 1302. Dante had supported the White Guelphs during the war, was initially fined and given a two-year exile, but when he refused to pay the fine his sentence was extended to exile for life. This is how he ended up in Ravenna, where he lived for twenty years. The journey to Venice was his last journey. He was sent there on a mission regarding smuggled salt. The mission failed,[11] and Dante caught malaria on the way home, possibly in the Comacchio marshlands. He died in Ravenna on 13 or 14 September the same year.

San Polo, 2170 Campo San Polo

Campo Sant'Agostin

At the end of the fifteenth century, Venice had more than two hundred printing presses, all of which helped in the spread of books throughout the Republic. Campo Sant'Agostin is where the Aldine printing press began in 1494. It printed popular Latin and Greek texts. Michelle Lovric's novel *The Floating Book* (2003) explores the world of late fifteenth-century presses.

Monument to Dante Alighieri in Florence.
Tommaso Lizzul

SANTA CROCE

The district of Santa Croce is where the train arrives and is the only area in Venice where cars are allowed. In this sense it's a link between the mainland and the city of the lagoon. It's named after the Church of Santa Croce, which was demolished in the early nineteenth century.

Palazzo Soranzo Capello and the Aspern Papers

Henry James used Palazzo Soranzo Capello as inspiration for the villa in his novella *The Aspern Papers* (1888), also on account of its secret walled garden, although all gardens in Venice tended to be walled as protection against high water. In James' novella, the narrator (we never find out his name) promises to take care of the garden for Miss Bordereau and her niece, and in this way makes his acquaintance with the two ladies. Claire Clairmont, half-sister of Mary Shelley, who lost her daughter to Byron in Venice, is said to have been

Santa Croce. Kristina Maikova

the inspiration for Miss Bordereau. We find out that Miss Bordereau had a love affair with a famous poet. She is now well into her later years, lives in the palazzo and guards her correspondence between herself and the writer. These are the papers that the narrator so desperately wants, and these are the papers he will never have.

Ramo Quinti Gallion O del Pezzetto, 770

Santa Croce. Ekaterina Belova

6
ISLANDS

As the city of Venice consolidated its position as one of the most powerful maritime republics the world has seen, the islands stayed at a slower pace, with traditional trades such as glassmaking on Murano and lacemaking on Burano. For the people who lived there, crossing the lagoon was often a major event and involved a journey of several hours. The first tourists started to explore the islands around the middle of the nineteenth century. From the latter part of the nineteenth century, it was quite common to see steamboats making their way out to the Lido amidst the traditional gondolas and rowing boats, filled with both local people and tourists. This new way of travelling could take more people to the islands in less time. As a result,

Island of Murano. Yasonya

Island of Torcello. Adobestock 18042011

a visit to the Lido became a popular day out. It provoked outrage amongst writers who had visited Venice and returned to see the steamboats going off to the Lido. Ruskin had a literary fit and complained that the noise of the steamboats stopped him from being able to write. He was appalled by the 'gimcrack lure of cheap tourism'. Then in 1881, the first *vaporetto* boat made its way down the Grand Canal. It was all a stark contrast to the windswept, desolate island that Byron and Shelley rode along when Shelley went to Venice in 1818. Of course, times change and life moves on, but it's hard not to feel a wave of nostalgia for something you can only read about when you line up to take your place on the boats out to the islands today. The freedom and the wildness were known by some at least.

Murano

Murano is famous all over the world for its glass production, and a visit to the glassmakers has always been popular. Thomas Coryat visited Murano, where he had a go at glassblowing and ate oysters.[1] Tracy Chevalier's

Above: *Glass shop in Murano.* skyoftexas

Below: *Glass blowing in Murano.* EMrpize

The Glassmaker (2024) begins in 1486 when glassmakers were highly paid and respected, Venice was a half-hour boat journey away from the mainland, and the glassmakers could never leave Venice for risk of taking the secrets of the glassmakers out of Murano. The heyday of Murano glass ended with the fall of the Republic, when the Austrians imposed taxes, and Murano no longer had the monopoly on glass throughout Europe. In Chevalier's book we see how glassmakers must learn to adapt right up to the twenty-first century and during times of Covid. It's a magnificent journey through time and history to get a real insight into the Murano glass industry but also into the history of Venice. Marina Fiorato's *The Glassblower of Murano* (2008) also brings this world to life during the Venetian Republic, with spies and informants and the Council of Ten who controlled all.

Lazzaretto Vecchio is a small island to the west of Murano. It's the island that is described in *The Glassmaker* (2024) as a place where people with the plague were sent. Outbreaks happened in Italy from the fourteenth century right up until the eighteenth, and because Venice was a port it was more at risk. It was quite common for visitors to be quarantined on their arrival in the

Plague doctor costume at Venice carnival. crisfotolux

city at Lazzaretto Vecchio. The arrival of the plague was what everyone feared, along with the plague doctor. He wore a bird-like mask that contained herbs that were supposed to protect him, a long black cape and gloves, and a black hat. He arrives in *The Glassmaker* (2024) when the plague arrives on Murano and within the central character's own family. *In the Company of the Courtesan* (2006), Murano is also where La Draga, the strange creature who cures the courtesan Fiammetta, comes from but guards her secrets closely.

Lido

'Brighter than burning gold'[2] is how Shelley described the evening skies at the Lido. He was writing about his

evening rides with Byron along the beach in his poem *Julian and Maddalo* (1824). Byron was a regular at the Lido Island and often rode along the beach from Alberoni, where he kept his horses. It's a wonderful image that encapsulates the freedom in which the Romantic poets believed. The subtext of course was that Mary Shelley had been on her way to Venice with their baby daughter Clara who was very ill and died in Mary's arms when they arrived. They buried Clara here on the Lido Island. When Mary returned years later in the 1840s with her only surviving son, she was unable to find the grave.[3]

The Lido started to become popular with foreign visitors during the 1880s, when families such as the Astors and

Cycling along the canal near Malamocco, Lido di Venezia. Andrea Vismara

Desboroughs started to spend holidays there. If before they had spent their holidays along the French Riviera or the 'Riviera' as it was known and everyone knew which one they meant, they were now also choosing Venice. The Venice Film Festival started in 1932. It was the first of its kind in Europe as the Cannes festival came later in 1946, and every year it's still Venice's most glamorous event. Colm Tóibín, in his essay about lockdown in Venice, writes that the best part of the Lido is the journey there and back. He says that it's all 'pretty ordinary over there' and he can feel no literary ghosts.[4] I'll leave it up to you to decide. Head to Malamocco, the old fishing village, which was the ancient seat of government.

Suntans and Chanel Pyjamas

During the 1920s the Lido took off as a place for the fashionable sets from all over Europe. Coco Chanel had made suntans fashionable when she got off a boat in Cannes sporting one. She'd been cruising the Mediterranean and caught too much sun, and suddenly everyone wanted a tan. In response, she designed a one-piece swimming costume made from woven bouclé fabric and so brought swimwear up to date. The Lido became the place to be with its eternal party atmosphere. The fashion for beach pyjamas also took off. *Harper's Bazaar* ran an advert for the Venice Lido with its sunshine and pyjamas, *Town and Country*'s society pages showed people there in the clothing, including Chanel ones.[5] Evelyn Waugh looks back to these days in a letter to Laura Waugh, where he talks about everyone being in pyjamas all morning in Venice before the war.[6]

Edith Wharton was critical about the crowd that descended on the Lido every summer. Lady Wrench, in *The Children* (1928), lamented the fact that all the smart set were taking the bathing tents, including the Duke of Mendip, who had one of theirs.[7] In the same novel, the parents are 'jazzing in Venice',[8] spending their summer between the Lido and ice creams at Florian's in St Mark's Square. The children are left to

Venice at the beginning of the nineteenth century. everettovrk

their own devices before being sent to Switzerland, a world where 'evidently the Lido Palace values were different'.[9] Henry James referred to it as the 'cockney village'.[10]

The Grand Excelsior Hotel and the Grand Hotel Des Bains

There were two main hotels at the Lido, each of which attracted a slightly different crowd. The Grand Hotel Excelsior opened in 1908 and was grand in scale, and famous for parties on the beach. The nightclub Chez Vous opened in the 1920s and became the place where all the smart set went. Grand Hotel des Bains opened a year later, was slightly more refined and as a result attracted a more refined type of people, including German writer Thomas Mann and Coco Chanel. It remained one of the popular hotels over the years, although Evelyn Waugh wasn't so keen. When he wrote to his friend Ann Fleming in April 1962, he complained about the speedboats, which he thought should be kept at the Excelsior and not allowed to visit the main islands.[11] The people who were in the speedboats, however, were evidently having a wonderful time.

Thomas Mann and Death in Venice

Thomas Mann was staying on the Lido at the Hotel des Bains in 1911 when he

Venice Lido. P.S. DESIGN

saw a young Polish boy. It was then that he had the idea that became his novella *Death in Venice* (1912). It's the story of a German writer who comes to Venice and meets Tazio, a Polish boy, who he then falls in love with. The book was set at the hotel, and Luchino Visconti's film *Morte a Venezia* (*Death in Venice*) was filmed inside the hotel in 1971.

The Bright Young Things

This group of young aristocrats, socialites and bohemians and the people that surrounded them belonged to the generation between the wars. Some of them were also writers, such as Nancy Mitford, one of the six Mitford sisters. They spent their lives in London, various country homes, Paris and the French Riviera, and came to Venice every year and to the Lido, along with a whole host of the international jet set from the United States and all over Europe. Theirs was the atmosphere that defined the time, also known as the Jazz Age. It was a period of excess and high festivities that continued through into the 1930s; all sex, drugs and jazz, with women in flapper dresses and bobbed hair. Everyone was out to enjoy themselves and of course each other's husbands and wives. American gossip columnist Elsa Maxwell was incredibly influential in it all. Whether in New York, Paris,

London, Monte Carlo or Venice, she was the party queen. If Elsa checked into a hotel, you knew that a party was about to happen.[12] Noël Coward personified the London scene, while American composer Cole Porter, also well-known for his extravagant parties, was another important figure on the scene. They brought Venice Lido to life, Cecil Beaton photographed them, and Evelyn Waugh wrote the novel *Vile Bodies* (1930), a satire on the bright young things and Mayfair during the 1920s. He dedicated it to his muse, Diana Mitford.

Lady Diana Cooper

'Today has been typically wonderful. Luncheon on two wide fishing boats about a hundred yards from the beach … Music on board, and spaghetti.'[13] This is Lady Diana Cooper's diary entry, of 30 August 1931, published in the second volume of her three-book autobiography *The Light of Common Day* (1959). She writes from Palazzo Mocenigo along the Grand Canal, where American socialite Laura Corrigan hosts her parties, news of which is reported in the US newspapers. Cooper was a socialite, actor and memoirist, daughter of the 7th Duke of Rutland and pre-Raphaelite artist Violet Lindsay, and was very good friends with Noel Coward, Nancy Mitford and Wallis Simpson. She was married

Do as Lady Diana Cooper did and head for a plate of spaghetti in Venice. kityayya

to Duff Cooper and friend of Elsa Maxwell, although Duff was slightly less impressed by Elsa. D.H. Lawrence used Lady Diana Cooper as inspiration for Lady Artemis Hooper in *Aaron's Rod* (1922), who Lawrence wrote as an aristocratic lady who got what she wanted, and who lay in bed after falling through the window of her taxi. Cooper's autobiographies, which take in trips to Venice, give a real insight into this world of luxury, cruises, and road trips in a Fiat that was spotted in Venice and bought for the occasion.[14]

Evelyn Waugh

English writer Evelyn Waugh first went to Venice in 1929 on the way back from a trip to Malta. He was friends with Lady Diana Cooper and her husband Duff, Nancy Mitford and Elsa Maxwell. Waugh met up with Lady Diana when he went to Venice in August 1932. He had previously met her in London and theirs would be a long and lasting friendship. The visit provided him with plenty of material that he would later use in his novel *Brideshead Revisited* (1945),[15] which is partially set in Venice. Charles Ryder goes off with his friend Sebastian Flyte to Venice, where Flyte is living with his mistress Cara. The mistress, surprisingly for Charles, turns out to be a respectable middle-aged woman who reveals to him the true state of the relationship between Lord and Lady Marchmain. The two young men spend two weeks being tourists in Venice with Cara and a guide. 'I was drowning in honey, stingless,' Charles tells us, and somehow, we know exactly what he means.

In 1960 Waugh wrote a piece about Venice for the *Daily Mail*, and in a letter to his friend Ann Fleming on 17 February 1960, he writes of how he was having a 'ripping time at the expense of the Daily Mail'. It was the first time he had seen Venice in January. It was 'exquisitely melancholy, misty, empty, silent'.[16] The piece ran with the title: *Sinking, Shadowed and Sad – The Last Glory of Europe.* In a letter to Nancy Mitford, he writes of how he had a lovely winter holiday but had to pay for it all with some 'very uncongenial articles for the Daily Mail'.

D.H. Lawrence and Venice

Lawrence could never be classed as a bright young thing, and nor was he enamoured with Venice, although he

Grand Canal and Basilica Santa Maria della Saluta. sborisov

lived in Italy during three periods of his life. In his poem *Pomegranate* (1932), he called it 'an abhorrent, green, slippery city/Whose Doges were old, and had ancient eyes'. In *Lady Chatterley's Lover*, Connie goes to Venice with her sister Hilda to cover the fact that she might already be pregnant because of her affair with Mellors, the gamekeeper. The idea is that she has an affair in Venice so that she can cover up the identity of the baby's true father. Venice fails to impress her, just as it failed to impress Lawrence. She looks over at Venice and sees a city 'built of money, blossomed of money; and dead with money'.[17] Lawrence criticised the Lido and compared the sun worshippers to piles of seals who were there only for mating. All the gondolas and ices and steamers and cocktails and more is simply 'too much enjoyment, altogether far too much enjoyment!'[18] In a letter to Lady Cynthia Asquith on 23 October 2013, he asks her if going to Venice in a week was too much. 'And did it stink?' he continues. 'Lord, but how Italy can stink.'[19] Luckily, he has a slightly more favourable opinion of Lerici in the Golfo della Spezia, from where he writes.

The Second World War

At the same time fascism was slowly rearing its head. Mussolini marched on Rome in 1922, and the fascist takeover

A vaporetto or steamer in Venice near the Rialto bridge. AlexAnton

began. During the war everyone went back home, and in September 1943 Venice was occupied along with the rest of northern Italy. *The Venice Sketchbook* (2021) by Rhys Bowen tells the story of a young Englishwoman who is stranded in Venice during the Second World War, while Siobhan Daiko's *The Girl from Venice* (2021) follows the story of Lidia who joins the partisan fighters up in the mountains.

After the War

After the war, the jet set returned to the Lido, and journalist and writer Elsa Maxwell continued as queen of the Lido scene, orchestrating the entertainment. Her parties were legendary, and her friends included Wallis Simpson, Marilyn Monroe, Aristotle Onassis, and Maria Callas, with whom it is said she was in unrequited love.

San Lazzaro Degli Armeni

The small island of San Lazzaro is in front of the Lido Island, and home to the monastery of the Armenian monks and their library, which has 170,000 volumes and 4,500 manuscripts from all over the world. Armenian monks originally came here at the beginning of the eighteenth century, and this is where Byron came to study the Armenian language when he was in Venice at the beginning of the nineteenth century. He admitted he found the language difficult but still spent about six months coming here to try to learn it. Robert Browning, American poet Henry Wadsworth Longfellow and Marcel Proust have all visited the island and its monastery. It is one of the most important Armenian centres in the world.

Pellestrina

The island of Pellestrina to the south of the Lido Island towards Chioggia is the setting for Martin Cruz Smith's novel *The Girl from Venice* (2016). A fisherman from the island rescues a Jewish girl from the city at the end of the Second World War, and the life of the fishermen on this island in the south of the Venetian lagoon is brought to life alongside the events of the end of the war. Come here for long sandy beaches, coloured houses and the local seafood.

San Lazzaro degli Armeni. ChiccoDodiFC

Island of Pellestrina. Morenovel

Island of Torcello. Artur Bogacki

Torcello

Ruskin, Henry James, George Sand, Ernest Hemingway, Nancy Mitford and Daphne du Maurier all loved it here on this quiet island in the north-east of the lagoon. It's rich in Byzantine architecture and archaeological treasures, and home to the famous Locanda Cipriani, which has hosted several writers over the years.

Locanda Cipriani

Giuseppe Cipriani, owner of Harry's Bar in San Marco, took over a small shop that sold wine and oil in 1934, and turned it into a *locanda* or inn with a restaurant and a few tasteful rooms. It had a garden and overlooked the island's two churches. Famous writers who came here included Ernest Hemingway and Somerset Maugham, while Nancy Mitford stayed here for two months in 1956. Hemingway stayed here in autumn 1948 and spent the whole of November writing his novel *Across the River and into the Trees* (1950). He used to go duck shooting with Giuseppe Cipriani, owner of the *locanda*.

Piazza Santa Fosca, 29

Nancy Mitford

Nancy Mitford spent almost two months here at the Locanda Cipriani in July 1956. By this time, she was a best-selling and respected writer. She'd started out as a regular contributor to the magazine *The Lady* and had written two highly successful novels based on her life, *In Pursuit of Love* (1945) and *Love in a Cold Climate* (1949). She was now here in 1956 to write a book about Voltaire's seventeen-year-long love affair with Emille, the Marquise du Chatelet. In a letter to her friend Mrs Ham, who was holidaying on the Isle of Wight she called it 'the most perfect place for work I ever was in',[20] and writes of how the waiters continuously try to give her more food. Gill Johnson writes about the time she spent with Mitford in her memoir about the year she spent in Venice in 1957 and looks after the two boys of the Brandolini d'Adda family. Gill meets her at the Lido and invites her join her and the boys at the beach. Mitford was viewed as an equal of writers such as Evelyn Waugh and Anthony Powell, and Johnson writes how: 'I was in the presence of a literary lioness.'[21]

Daphne Du Maurier

Daphne du Maurier had lunch in the restaurant at the Locanda Cipriani in September 1965 and watched a pair of elderly twins at a table in the restaurant, one of whom was blind. Her husband Tommy had died in March that year, and she was in Venice with her sister Jeanne. It gave her an idea, and the idea became her short story *Don't Look Now* (1971), where there is a couple in a restaurant observing the elderly twins and imagining what they are doing on Torcello. It's a chilling tale of a couple who go to Venice to try to get over the death of their daughter. In contrast to the international jet set, du Maurier was a private person who led a very private life in her home in Fowey on the south coast of Cornwall. She also went to Venice in February 1952. She should have gone to Balmoral as her husband had been made Treasurer to the Duke of Edinburgh, but the visit was cancelled as Tommy had hurt his arm and was unable to go hunting as planned. So off she went to Venice instead as a guest of the retired British Consul of Geneva Ronald Armstrong, with whom she had developed a friendship. It was all perfectly innocent. He was gay, twenty years older than she was, and therefore the perfect companion to give the good company she needed at the time.[22] *Ganymede* (1959) is another story set in Venice, in which a retired professor is on holiday in Venice when he falls for a young Italian waiter. Venice is the perfect place for this tense and disturbing tale.

POSTSCRIPT

On the islands of the Venetian lagoon, we go back to the origins of Venice, where as early as the fourth century, people lived on the island of Torcello. When invaders came down from the north, the people of Veneto fled to the lagoon. Sometimes they went home again and sometimes they stayed and adapted their ways of life that they'd brought from the mainland to the marshes of the islands in the lagoon. They built boats and thatched

Torcello with the mountains in the distance. Madeleine Deaton

An aerial view of Venice. Frimufilms

dwellings and lived on a diet of fish and seawater.[1] As Ruskin writes in his book *The Stones of Venice* (1851), 'Thirteen hundred years ago the gray moorland looked as it does this day, and the purple mountains stood as radiantly in the deep distances of evening'.[2]

LIST OF WORKS INCLUDED

Alighieri, D., *The Divine Comedy*, 1321

Andersen, H.C., *What the Moon Saw*, 1840

Bedford, S., *Pleasures and Landscapes*, 2003

Berendt, J., *The City of Falling Angels*, 2006

Bowen, R., *The Venice Sketchbook*, 2021

Brodsky, J., *Watermark: An Essay on Venice*, 1989

Brown, H., *Life on the Lagoons*, 1884

Browning, R., *A Toccata of Galuppi's*, 1855

Browning, R., *Asolando*, 1889

Browning, R., *De Gustibus*, 1855

Browning, R., *Sordello*, 1883

Byatt, A.S., *Peacock and Vine: Fortuny and Morris in Life and at Work*, 2016

Byron, George Gordon, *Beppo: A Venetian Story*, 1818

Byron, George Gordon, *Childe Harold's Pilgrimage*, 1812

Byron, George Gordon, *Don Juan*, 1819

Byron, George Gordon, *Manfred*, 1817

Byron, George Gordon, *Ode on Venice*, 1819

Casanova, G., *The Memoirs*, 1822

Chevalier, T., *The Glass Maker*, 2024

Coles, P., *The Politics of Washing: Real Life in Venice*, 2013

Constable, H., *The Instrumentalist*, 2024

Cooper, D., *The Light of Common Day*, 1959

Coryat, T., *Coryat's Crudities*, 1611

Dacre, C., *Zofloya, or, The Moor*, 1806

Daiko, S., *The Girl from Venice*, 2023

David, E., *Italian Food*, 1954

De Blasi, M., *A Thousand Days in Venice*, 2003

De Pizan, C., *The Book of the City of Ladies*, 1405

Di Robilant, A., *A Venetian Affair: A True Tale of Forbidden Love in the 18th Century*, 2003

Di Robilant, A., *Lucia, A Venetian Life in the Age of Napoleon*, 2008

Dibdin, M., *Dead Lagoon*, 1994

Dickens, C., *Pictures from Italy*, 1846

Du Maurier, D., *Ganymede*, 1959

Du Maurier, D., *Don't Look Now*, 1971

Dunant, S., *In the Company of the Courtesan*, 2013

Elkin, L., *Flâneuse: Women Walk the City in Paris, New York, Tokyo, Venice and London*, 2016

Fiorato, M., *The Glassblower of Murano*, 2007

Fonte, M., *The Merits of Women: Wherein is Clearly Revealed Their Nobility and Their Superiority to Men*, 1600

Goethe, J.W., *Voyage in Italy*, 1816

Guggenheim, P., *Confessions of an Art Addict*, 1960

Hemingway, E., *Across the River and into the Trees*, 1950

Hemingway, E., *A Farewell to Arms*, 1929

Highsmith, P., *The Talented Mr Ripley*, 1955

Highsmith, P., *Those Who Walk Away*, 1967

Highsmith, P., *Winter in Venice*, published online at www.theoldie.co.uk, first accessed 28 July 2024

James, H., *A London Life*, 1888

James, H., *Italian Hours*, 1909

James, H., *Letters from the Palazzo Barbaro (Pushkin Collection)*, 1998

James, H., *The Aspern Papers*, 1888

James, H., *The Innocents Abroad*, 1869

James, H., *The Wings of the Dove*, 1902

Johnson, G., *Love from Venice: A Golden Summer on the Grand Canal*, 2024

Jones, P.G., *To Venice with Love: A Midlife Adventure*, 2019

Lawrence, D.H., *Lady Chatterley's Lover*, 1928

Lawrence, D.H., *Pomegranate*, 1932

Lee, V., *A Wicked Voice*, 1890

Lee, V., *Studies of the Eighteenth Century in Italy*, 1880

Leon, D., *Death at La Fenice*, 1994

Leon, D., *My Venice and other Essays*, 2014

Lovric, M., *Carnevale*, 2015

Lovric, M., *The Floating Book*, 2015

Lovric, M., *The Water's Daughter*, 2020

Lovric, M., *The Wishing Bones*, 2019

Lovric, M., *The Undrowned Child*, 2009

Mann, T., *Death in Venice*, 1912

Marinelli, L., *The Nobility and Excellence of Women and the Defects and Vices of Men*, 1600

Melville, L. and Montagu, M., *Lady Mary Wortley Montagu, her Life and Letters (1689–1762)*, 1925

Middleton, T., *Women Beware Women*, 1657

Montague, Lady Mary Wortley, *Lady Mary Wortley Montague, Her Life and Letters (1689–1762)*, edited by Melville, L., 2023

Morgan, Lady (Sydney), *Italy*, 1821

Morris, J., *Jan Morris Remembers the Magic of Venice, Now and Then*, 21 December 2015, in Vanity Fair, www.vanityfair.com, first accessed 20 October 2024

Morris, J., *Let Her Sink*, 20 July 1975, in the *New York Times*, www.nytimes.com/1975/07/20/archives/let-her-sink-a-longtime-lover-of-venice-that-flamboyant-shell.html, first accessed 20 October 2024

Morris, J., *Venice*, 1960

Nardin, M.O., *Beneath the Lion's Wings*, 2018

Pound, E., *A Lume Spento*, 1908

Quick, B., *Vivaldi's Virgins*, 2007

Radcliffe, A., *The Mysteries of Udolpho*, 1794

Rogers, S., *Italy, a Poem*, 1822

Ruskin, J., *The Stones of Venice*, 1851

Rylands, J.T., *Across the Bridge of Sighs: More Venetian Stories*, 2007

Rylands, J.T., *Venetian Stories*, 2004

Sansovino, F., *Venetia*, 1581

Shakespeare, W., *Othello*, 1622

Shakespeare, W., *The Merchant of Venice*, 1600

Shelley, M., *Rambles in Germany and Italy in 1840, 1842 and 1843*, 1844

Shelley, P.B., *History of a Six Weeks' Tour, through a part of France, Switzerland and Germany, and Holland: with Letters Descriptive of a Sail round the Lake of Geneva, and the Glaciers of Chamouni*, 1817

Shelley, P.B., *Julian and Maddalo: A Conversation*, 1824

Smith, D., *The Honeymoon*, 2016

Smith, M.C., *The Girl from Venice*, Simon and Schuster, 2016

Spark, M., *Territorial Rights*, 1979

Spark, M., *Venice in Fall and Winter*, 25 October 1981 in the *New York Times*, archive.nytimes.com/www.nytimes.com/books/01/03/11/specials/spark-venice.html, first accessed September 2024

Starke, M., *Letters from Italy, between the years 1792 and 1798*, 1800

Starke, M., *Travels on the Continent: Written for the Use and Particular Information of Travellers*, 1820

Twain, M., *The Innocents Abroad*, 1869

Waugh, E., *Brideshead Revisited*, 1945

Wharton, E., *A Venetian's Night Entertainment*, 1929

Wharton, E., *Italian Backgrounds*, 1905

Wharton, E., *The Children*, 1928

Wharton, E., *The Glimpses of the Moon*, 1922

Wharton, E., *The Verdict*, 1908

Whittaker, D. and Coryate, T., *Most Glorious and Peerless Venice, Observations of Thomas Coryate (1608)*, Wavestone Press, 2013

Woolf, V., *The Diary of Virginia Woolf Volume 4 1931–1935*, 1979

Wordsworth, W., *On the Extinction of the Venetian Republic*, 1807

Zaran, C., *Italy*, 2023

BIBLIOGRAPHY

Acton, H., *Nancy Mitford: The Biography*, 1975

Ackroyd, P., *Shakespeare: The Biography*, Vintage Books, 2006

Andersen, H.C., *What the Moon Saw: And Other Tales*, 1866

Berrino, A., *Storia del Turismo in Italia*, Società editrice il Mulino, 2011

Browning, E.B., *The Letters of Elizabeth Barrett Browning*, edited by Kenyon, F.C., 1898

Cooper, D., *The Light of Common Day*, 1959

Dammann, G., *Enlightenment on Casanova's Sexual Preferences*, 27 June 2008, www.theguardian.com/books/2008/jun/27/biography.history, first accessed 1 October 2024

Di Robilant, A., *Autumn in Venice: Ernest Hemingway and His Last Muse*, 2018

Eade, P., *Evelyn Waugh: A Life Revisited*, 1945

Forster, M., *Daphne Du Maurier: The Secret Life of the Renowned Storyteller*, 1993

Freedman, H., *Shylock's Venice: The Remarkable History of Venice's Jews and the Ghetto*, 2024

Gransard, M., *Venice: A Literary Guide for Travellers*, Tauris Parke, 2019

Hay, D., *Young Romantics: The Shelleys, Byron and other Tangled Lives*, Bloomsbury UK, 2011

Highsmith, P., *Her Diaries and Notebooks*, W&N, 2021

Holmes, R., *Sylvia Pankhurst: Natural Born Rebel*, 2021

Hutton, L., *Literary Landmarks of Venice*, 1896

Kenny, D., *Between Me and My Real Self: On Vernon Lee*, 2018 www.theparisreview.org/blog/2018/04/03/between-me-and-my-real-self-on-vernon-lee, first accessed 25 October 2024

Lassels, R., *The Voyage of Italy*, 1670

Lawrence, D.H., *The Selected Letters of D H Lawrence*, 1958

Lee, H., *Edith Wharton*, 2008

Littlewood, I., *Venice: A Literary Companion*, 1992

MacCarthy, F., *Peacock and Vine by A.S. Byatt review: Mariano Fortuny and William Morris, masters of design*, The Guardian, 2016

McCarthy, M., *Venice Observed*, 1963

Mackrell, J., *The Unfinished Palazzo*, 2017

Moers, E. ,*The Letters of Virginia Woolf*, New York Times, 23 November 1975

Mroz, J., *How NJ Native Donna Leon Became an International Bestselling Author, 26* May 2022, in *New Jersey Monthly*, www.newjerseymonthly.com, first accessed 1 October 2024

New York Times, 'Ezra Pound Is Buried with Simple Rites at Island Cemetery in Venice', 4 November 1972, *New York Times*, first accessed 1 September 2024

Parkinson, J., 'When pyjamas ruled the fashion world', 31 January 2016, BBC New Magazine online

Prodger, M., 'John Ruskin's marriage: what really happened', *The Guardian*, 2013, first accessed 2 August 2024

Rendell, M., *The Grand Tour*, 2022

Rosenthal, M., *The Honest Courtesan*, 1992

Ross, L., *Portrait of Hemingway*, 1961

Saikia, R., *The Venice Lido: A Blue Guide Travel Monograph*, 2011

Scarpa, T., *Venice is a Fish*, 2000

Seymour, M., *Mary Shelley*, 2002

Shelley, P.B., *The Letters of Percy Bysshe Shelley, Volume 2: Shelley in Italy*, edited by Jones, F., Oxford Clarendon Press, 1964

Staggs, S., *Inventing Elsa Maxwell: how an Irrepressible Nobody Conquered High Society, Hollywood, the Press and the World*, 2012

Strachan, M., *The Life and Adventures of Thomas Coryate*, Oxford University Press, 1962

Tóibín, C., 'Diary: Alone in Venice', *London Review of Books* Vol. 44 No. 22

Waugh, E., *The Letters of Evelyn Waugh*, edited by Amory, M. 1989

Wutrich, N., *Isabella's Bookworm Friendship with Vernon Lee*, 2022 www.gardnermuseum.org/blog/isabellas-bookworm-friendship-vernon-lee, first accessed 25 October 2024

Zorzi, P., *A Venezia Lucean le Stelle*, 2023

ENDNOTES

Preface

1. James, H., *Italian Hours*, 1909.

Historical Notes

1. Morris, J., *Venice*, 1960.
2. Ibid.
3. Wharton. E., *Italian Backgrounds*, 1905.
4. Rendell, M., *The Grand Tour*, Shire Publications, 2022.
5. Ibid.
6. Di Robilant, A., *A Venetian Affair: A True Tale of Forbidden Love in the 18th Century*, Alfred a Knopf Inc., 2003.
7. Berrino, A., *Storia del Turismo in Italia*, Società editrice il Mulino, 2011.
8. Morris, J., *Venice*, 1960.

When to Go

1. Bedford, S., *Pleasures and Landscapes*, 2003.
2. Waugh, E., *The Letters of Evelyn Waugh*, 1989.
3. Leon, D.
4. Highsmith, P., *The Talented Mr Ripley*, 1955.

Arriving in Venice

1. Shelley, M., *Rambles in Germany and Italy in 1840, 1842 and 1843* (1844).
2. Twain, M., *The Innocents Abroad*, 1869.
3. Starke, M., *Travels on the Continent: Written for the Use and Particular Information of Travellers*, 1820.
4. Morgan, Lady (Sydney), *Italy*, 1821.
5. Ibid.

North of the Grand Canal

1. Guggenheim, P., *Out of this Century*, Universe Books, 1946.
2. James, H., *The Aspern Papers*, 1888.
3. Spark, M., *Territorial Rights*, MacMillan, 1979.
4. Johnson, G., *Love from Venice: A Golden Summer on the Grand Canal*, Hodder and Stoughton, 2024.
5. James, H., *Italian Hours*, 1909.
6. James, H., *The Aspern Papers*, 1888.
7. Dammann, G., *Enlightenment on Casanova's Sexual Preferences*, 27 June 2008, www.theguardian.com/books/2008/jun/27/biography.history, first accessed 1 October 2024.
8. Spark, M., *Territorial Rights*, MacMillan, 1979.

9. Saikia, R., *The Venice Lido*, Blue Guides Ltd, 2011.
10. Ibid.
11. Hay, D., *Young Romantics: The Shelleys, Byron and other Tangled Lives*, Bloomsbury UK, 2011.
12. Ibid.
13. Melville, L. and Montagu. M., *Lady Mary Wortley Montagu, her Life and Letters (1689–1762)*, Hutchinson, London, 1925.
14. Ibid.
15. Lee, H., *Edith Wharton*, Vintage, 2008.
16. Ibid.
17. Wutrich, N., *Isabella's Bookworm Friendship with Vernon Lee*, 2022, www.gardnermuseum.org/blog/isabellas-bookworm-friendship-vernon-lee first accessed 25 October 2024.
18. Kenny, D., *Between Me and My Real Self: On Vernon Lee*, 2018, www.theparisreview.org/blog/2018/04/03/between-me-and-my-real-self-on-vernon-lee, first accessed 25 October 2024.
19. Lee, V., *A Wicked Voice*, 1890.
20. Letter to Miss Mitford, 4 June 1851, in Browning, E.B., *The Letters of Elizabeth Barrett Browning*, edited by Kenyon, F.C., 1898.
21. Letter to John Kenyon, 7 July 1851, in Browning, E.B., *The Letters of Elizabeth Barrett Browning*, edited by Kenyon, F.C., 1898.
22. MacCarthy, F., *Peacock and Vine by A S Byatt review: Mariano Fortuny and William Morris, masters of design, The Guardian*, 2016.
23. Gransard, M., *Venice: A Literary Guide for Travellers*, Tauris Parke, 2019.
24. Moers, E., *The Letters of Virginia Woolf*, New York Times, 23 November 1975.
25. Woolf, V., *The Diary of Virginia Woolf Volume 4 1931–1935*, 1979.
26. Gransard, M., *Venice: A Literary Guide for Travellers*, Tauris Parke, 2019.
27. Andersen, H.C., *What the Moon Saw: And Other Tales*, 1866.
28. Highsmith, P., *Her Diaries and Notebooks*, W&N, 2021.
29. Highsmith, P., *Winter in Venice*, published online at www.theoldie.co.uk, first accessed 28 July 2024.
30. Highsmith, P., *Her Diaries and Notebooks*, W&N, 2021.
31. Highsmith, P., *Those Who Walk Away*, 1967.
32. Zorzi, P., *A Venezia Lucean le Stelle*, Neri Pozzi, 2023.
33. Morris, J., *Venice*, 1960.
34. Morris, J., *Jan Morris Remembers the Magic of Venice, Now and Then*, 21 December 2015, in *Vanity Fair*, www.vanityfair.com, first accessed 20 October 2024.
35. Mroz, J., *How NJ Native Donna Leon Became an International Bestselling Author*, 26 May 2022 in *New Jersey Monthly*, www.newjerseymonthly.com, first accessed 1 October 2024.
36. Whittaker, D. and Coryate, T., *Most Glorious and Peerless Venice,*

Observations of Thomas Coryate (1608), Wavestone Press, 2013.

37. Ibid.
38. Strachan, M., *The Life and Adventures of Thomas Coryate*, Oxford University Press, 1962.
39. Whittaker, D. and Coryate, T., *Most Glorious and Peerless Venice, Observations of Thomas Coryate (1608)*, Wavestone Press, 2013.
40. Coryat, T., *Coryat's Crudities*, 1611.
41. Dunant, S., *In the Company of the Courtesan*, Virago, 2013.
42. Freedman, H., *Shylock's Venice: The Remarkable History of Venice's Jews and the Ghetto*, Bloomsbury Continuum, 2024.
43. Ackroyd, P., *Shakespeare: The Biography*, Vintage Books, 2006.
44. Hutton, L., *Literary Landmarks of Venice*, 1896.
45. Prodger, M., *John Ruskin's marriage: what really happened*, The Guardian, 2013, first accessed 2 August 2024.
46. Zorzi, P., *A Venezia lucean le Stelle*, 2023.
47. Dickens, C., *Pictures from Italy*, 1846.
48. Gransard, M., *Venice: A Literary Guide for Travellers*, 2019.
49. Dunant, S., *In the Company of the Courtesan*, 2013.
50. Mackrell, J., *The Unfinished Palazzo*, Thames & Hudson, 2017.
51. Ibid.
52. 'Ezra Pound is Buried with Simple Rites at Island Cemetery in Venice', 4 November 1972, *New York Times*, first accessed 1 September 2024.

South of the Grand Canal

1. Shelley, P.B., *The Letters of Percy Bysshe Shelley, Volume 2: Shelley in Italy,* edited by Jones, F., Oxford Clarendon Press, 1964.
2. Coryat, T., *Crudities*, 1611.
3. James, H., *The Innocents Abroad*, 1869.
4. Mackrell, J., *The Unfinished Palazzo*, 2017.
5. Di Robilant, A., *A Venetian Affair: A True Tale of Forbidden Love in the 18th Century*, Alfred a Knopf Inc., 2003.
6. Gransard, M., *Venice: A Literary Guide for Travellers*, Tauris Parke, 2019.
7. Zaran, C., *Italy*, 2023.
8. Saikia, R., *The Venice Lido: A Blue Guide Travel Monograph*, Blue Guides, 2011.
9. Holmes, R., *Sylvia Pankhurst: Natural Born Rebel*, Bloomsbury Publishing, 2021.
10. David, E., *Italian Food*, 1954.
11. Gransard, M., *Venice: A Literary Guide for Travellers*, Tauris Parke, 2019.

Islands

1. Coryat, T., *Crudities*, 1611.
2. Shelley, P., *Julian and Maddalo*, 1824.
3. Hay, D., *Young Romantics: The Shelleys, Byron and other Tangled Lives*, Bloomsbury UK, 2011.
4. Tóibín, C., 'Diary: Alone in Venice', *London Review of Books* Vol. 44 No. 22.

5. Parkinson, J., *When pyjamas ruled the fashion world*, 31 January 2016, BBC New Magazine online.
6. Waugh, E., *The Letters of Evelyn Waugh*, edited by Amory, M., 1989.
7. Wharton, E., *The Children*, 1928.
8. Ibid.
9. Ibid.
10. James, H., *Italian Hours*, 1909.
11. Waugh, E., *The Letters of Evelyn Waugh*, 1989.
12. Staggs, S., *Inventing Elsa Maxwell: How an Irrepressible Nobody Conquered High Society, Hollywood, the Press and the World*, St Martin's Press, 2012.
13. Cooper, D., *The Light of Common Day*, 1959.
14. Ibid.
15. Eade, P., *Evelyn Waugh: A Life Revisited*, 1945.
16. Waugh, E., *The Letters of Evelyn Waugh*, 1989.
17. Lawrence, D.H., *Lady Chatterley's Lover*, 1928.
18. Ibid.
19. Lawrence, D.H., *The Selected Letters of D H Lawrence*, 1958.
20. Acton, H., *Nancy Mitford: The Biography*, 1975.
21. Johnson, G., *Love from Venice: A Golden Summer on the Grand Canal*, Hodder & Stoughton, 2024.
22. Forster, M., *Daphne Du Maurier: The Secret Life of the Renowned Storyteller*, 1993.

Postscript

1. Morris, J., *Venice*, 1960.
2. Ruskin, J., *The Stones of Venice*, 1851.